BAD STORIES

BAD STORIES

What the Hell Just Happened
to Our Country

• • •

Steve Almond

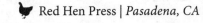 Red Hen Press | *Pasadena, CA*

This is a work of non-fiction, which is to say: a radically subjective version of events that objectively took place. I've changed a few names and identifying characteristics.

Book design by Mark E. Cull

Names: Almond, Steve, author.
Title: Bad stories : what the hell just happened to our country / Steve Almond.
Description: Pasadena, CA : Red Hen Press, 2018.
Identifiers: LCCN 2017043371 (print) | LCCN 2018004742 (ebook) | ISBN
    9781597092234 (ebook) | ISBN 9781597092265 (tradepaper)
Subjects: LCSH: Presidents—United States—Election—2016. | Trump, Donald,
    1946– | Political culture—United States. | Social values—United States.
    | Politics and literature—United States. | United States—Politics and
    government—2017–
Classification: LCC E911 (ebook) | LCC E911 .A56 2018 (print) | DDC
    973.933—dc23
LC record available at https://lccn.loc.gov/2017043371

Publication of this book is made possible in part through the financial support of Ann Beman, Deborah C. Schneider, and Jim Tilley.

The National Endowment for the Arts, the Los Angeles County Arts Commission, the Dwight Stuart Youth Fund, the Max Factor Family Foundation, the Pasadena Tournament of Roses Foundation, the Pasadena Arts & Culture Commission and the City of Pasadena Cultural Affairs Division, the City of Los Angeles Department of Cultural Affairs, the Audrey & Sydney Irmas Charitable Foundation, the Ahmanson Foundation, the Meta & George Rosenberg Foundation, the Kinder Morgan Foundation, the Allergan Foundation, the Riordan Foundation, and the Amazon Literary Partnership partially support Red Hen Press.

First Edition
Published by Red Hen Press
www.redhen.org
Printed in Canada

For Josie, Jude and Rosalie—
my storymakers, my loves

CONTENTS

BAD STORIES

Do you remember on the first page of dinner, mama?

The first page of dinner?

Didn't you know? We're all in a really long story.

—Rosalie Almond, age 3

Do you see the story? Do you see anything?

It seems to me I am trying to tell you a dream—

—Joseph Conrad

WATERGATE WAS ABOUT
A CORRUPT PRESIDENT

I can't claim to have lived through Watergate; I was all of five when it began. I only knew that something bad had happened in the adult world, that the president was in trouble and that his trouble seemed to grow worse with the appearance of the newspaper each morning.

I do remember watching Nixon resign, though. This would have been August of 1974. We were vacationing in Mendocino, on the north coast of California, where our family had spent the previous summer living, rather precariously, on a commune called The Land. A friend from The Land, the magnificently named Oak Sawyer, was visiting us when word arrived that Nixon was going to deliver a live address to the nation. Our little rental didn't have a TV, so Oak called a neighbor of his and everyone trooped over to this neat, middle-class home to watch the president say what he had to say.

It was the sort of impromptu viewing party that would be hard to imagine today. My parents and Oak were basically hippies. My brothers and I had hair down to our shoulders. Our host was a crew-cut gentleman who announced, rather gallantly, that he had voted for Nixon and regretted it.

The president appeared on screen, seated behind a desk in a dark suit. He read carefully from a stack of papers clutched before him, like a mortician droning out burial options. "Here come the tears," someone said.

Then, from the back of the room, I heard our mother say this: "They finally got the bastard."

I'm sure I was struck by her profanity. But what has stayed with me all these years is her tone. Beneath the contempt was a slender but distinct note of wonder. Someone (*they*) had done the impossible (*finally got the bastard*). It would take me several more years to put the pieces together.

◆ ◆ ◆

By junior high, I had seen *All the President's Men* in the theater, and dog-eared the paperback. I knew the Hollywood version of Watergate by heart, how a pair of intrepid reporters, using little more than coffee, typewriters, and the indomitable power of the free press, had brought down a corrupt president.

It's hard to explain to those who weren't alive in those years the holy glow that emanated from the word *journalist*. I spent fifteen years chasing that glow—as the editor of my high school and college papers, a slavish summer intern, and finally a full-time reporter.

But as I've grown older, and been relieved of various delusions about myself and our Fourth Estate, I am less dazzled by the specter of Woodward and Bernstein gum footing around Washington. What strikes me as the heart of Watergate is the public distress occasioned by the revelation that a president and his men would abuse their power. As evidence emerged of their corruption, citizens of all political persuasions, including our host in Mendocino, felt betrayed.

This sense of betrayal is what drove journalistic outlets to devote resources to the story, what led Congressional committees to launch inquiries, what spurred loyal aides to expose the president's deceits, what compelled the Supreme Court to order Nixon to release the Oval Office tapes that incriminated him, and what finally convinced Republicans in Congress to draw up Articles of Impeachment. A moral consensus emerged that truth and justice transcended partisanship. Our civic and political institutions upheld this standard.

The story of Watergate, then, wasn't ultimately about one man's debased behavior. It was about a nation's shared idealism.

The scandal led to a raft of reforms, intended to curb abuses of power and limit the influence of wealthy individuals, corporations, and lobbyists in political life. These measures have long enjoyed broad public support. By 2016, nearly all had been overturned in court, or allowed to lapse.

◆ ◆ ◆

The origins of Watergate reside in a simple burglary. Five men were arrested in the middle of the night for trying to bug the offices of the Democratic National Committee. When reporters learned of the arrests, they asked two questions: who had hired the burglars, and why? The dogged pursuit of these questions led to the exposure of a criminal espionage operation run out of the Oval Office.

In the early months of the 2016 campaign, burglars again broke into DNC headquarters. They too were looking for dirt that would help elect the Republican candidate. This time, the burglars were Russian hackers. And journalists were oddly unconcerned with who had hired them or why. Instead, they eagerly publicized every scrap of damning material made available to them.

These efforts were compounded by a slew of lurid and slanderous stories disseminated by Russian operatives and bots. The result was a potent smear campaign against the Democratic candidate, one engineered by the Kremlin, applauded (and perhaps abetted) by her Republican opponent, and carried out, in large measure, by our free press.

The burglary, in this case, led not to the resignation of a sitting president, but the election of a man widely regarded as ethically and mentally unfit for office, even by many of those who voted for him.

◆ ◆ ◆

This book originally carried a different (and rather more grandiose) subtitle: *Toward a Unified Theory of How It All Came Apart.* I ultimately chose a simpler phrase, one that captures something of the bewildment and exasperation so many Americans feel. But I mention that first subtitle to emphasize the nature of my undertaking. I'm not offering a single theory, or even a set of theories, as to how our democracy fell apart. I'm working *toward* a synthesis of theories. The ascension of Donald Trump to the presidency is certainly the impetus for this investigation. But it should not be mistaken for my subject.

In fact, I've been tracking the odd and lurching course of our democracy for most of my adult life. I've pursued this interest not as an academic—a historian or a political scientist—but as a reporter and, more recently, a fiction writer. That makes me a storyteller technically, though I feel more often like a woozy and puzzled student of the American story.

I've placed my faith in stories because I believe them to be the basic unit of human consciousness. The stories we tell, and the ones we absorb, are what allow us to pluck meaning from the rush of experience. Only through the patient interrogation of these stories can we begin to understand where we are and how we got here.

♦ ♦ ♦

In his elegant 2014 book, *Sapiens: A Brief History of Humankind*, the Israeli historian Yuval Noah Harari insists that our species came to dominate the world because we learned to cooperate flexibly in large numbers. This capacity, he contends, stems from our unique cognitive ability to believe in the imagined, to tell stories that extend our bonds beyond clan loyalties. Our larger systems of cooperation, whether spiritual, political, legal, or financial, require faith in a beautiful fiction known as the common good, the sort of mutual trust expressed in any trade agreement or currency.

For most of our history, humans relied upon folklore and religious parable to conceptualize a common good. But much of our progress as a species, Harari insists, is a function of cultures shifting from superstitious stories to verifiable ones, as happened during the Scientific Revolution of the 16th century. Our embrace of reason and empiricism has saved a lot of people from dying of illness and starvation. It has led to a standard of living within many precincts of the world that would have been unimaginable in previous epochs. It has not, however, changed the fact that we still choose the stories by which we construct reality.

What happens, then, when some of the stories we tell ourselves are bad, meaning fraudulent either by design or negligence? What happens when the stories we tell ourselves are frivolous? Or when we ignore stories that are too frightening to confront? What happens when we fall under the sway of stories intended to sow discord, to blunt our moral imaginations, to warp our fears into loathing and our mercy into vengeance? The principle argument of this book is that bad stories lead to bad outcomes.

I agree with Harari when he argues that our faith in stories has been integral to our survival as a species. But I also believe this capacity poses the central risk to our species, and that the 2016 election is an object lesson in just how much harm bad stories can inflict upon even the sturdiest democracy. A simpler way of saying this would be that bad stories arise from an unwillingness to take reality seriously. If bad stories become pervasive enough they create a new and darker reality.

◆ ◆ ◆

I realize I'm portraying this theory of bad stories as a kind of sophisticated literary analytic when it is, in fact, something closer to a rhetorical panic room. It was the only way I was able to explain to my young children how the adult population of the United States had selected as its leader a man most Americans recognized, intuitively, as a bully and a bullshitter.

Confronted by the searching gaze of my seven-year-old, Jude, I launched into a rambling theosophical lecture, the gist of which was this:

It's hard to be a human being because human beings have all these anxieties and unmet desires and aggressive impulses that we're constantly trying to manage. One way we do this is to tell stories that help us endure our difficult feelings and that remind us not to be ruled by our worst impulses. The most popular of these stories become our sacred texts.

For example (I told Jude) after Moses led the Jews out of Egypt, God called him to the top of a big mountain to give him two stone tablets with rules such as Don't Kill and Don't Lie and Don't Worship False Gods. But Moses spent a long time on the mountain and his followers got antsy, so they erected a big golden calf to worship. This made their lives more bearable.

Many years later, when the Jews again fell away from the word of God and became too consumed with power and money, a homeless rabbi named Jesus came along and began to preach a gospel of radical kindness. He insisted that the sick and poor were blessed and that the meek would inherit the Earth and even though he was murdered for these views, his followers came to believe that obedience to his teachings was the path to salvation. Jude had heard these stories and wanted to know if they were true. I said I didn't know exactly but that their truth wasn't really the point. A story didn't have to be true to produce a good outcome, to help people behave a little more kindly.

This brought my son right back to the central mystery he was pursuing: why had Trump, who did not behave kindly at all, won the election?

The main reason, I said, was because about half of all Americans didn't bother to vote.

"Why not?"

"They didn't believe it mattered, I guess."

"But what about the ones who did?" Jude said.

"Remember the people waiting around for Moses, the ones who began praying to the golden calf? Trump was like that golden calf. They felt helpless and he made them feel powerful."

My son let all this sit for a minute. Then he said, "There must be some wise people who voted for Trump. What stories do they believe?"

I looked at Jude for a good 30 seconds, probing the outer limits of my own tolerance, you might say. "They believe that he's a good businessman," I said carefully. "And they believe that he'll be able to get things done because he's never been a part of government."

"Doesn't government do things already?"

"Yes. But some people believe our government is broken."

"Is it?" Jude said.

"I don't think so," I said. "That's another one of our bad stories."

♦ ♦ ♦

The term *bad stories* is absurdly, perhaps dangerously, reductive. I could employ a more elegant term, *flawed* or *distorted*. But I'm going to stick with bad because it casts the widest net, and because it suggests a malignant motive as well as dubious content and damaging outcomes.

Stories don't fall from the clouds, after all. They are invented and refined and promoted by particular narrators with particular agendas. If we want to understand the bad stories that dominated the 2016 election, we have to examine the context from which they arose, and accept that our received version of history is often nothing more than the needlework of the powerful.

Consider this brief rewrite from the novelist Kurt Vonnegut: "As children we were taught to memorize [1492] . . . as the year people began living full and imaginative lives on the continent of North America. Actually, people had been living full and imaginative lives on the continent of America for hundreds of years before that. 1492 was simply the year sea pirates began to rob, cheat, and kill them."

The same revisionism should be applied to the story of our own national origin, with its noble assertion that *all men are created equal.* We all know the author of those words was an aristocrat who owned human beings, and that our founding documents were designed to safeguard this peculiar institution.

Slavery, in turn, was constructed upon another bad story that wealthy colonists began telling long before Thomas Jefferson came along. Poor people vastly outnumbered the rich: European immigrants, slaves, and indentured servants of European and African heritage. If these populations recognized their mutual economic interests and banded together—as they did during Bacon's Rebellion, for instance— the ruling class was toast.

So landed settlers came up with the story of race, and specifically the concept of whiteness, which held that all European immigrants in the colonies, regardless of class, were bound by a pigmentary alliance that made them inherently superior to anyone with darker skin. This alliance didn't make an indentured servant any less indentured. It merely granted them what W.E.B. Du Bois would later call the "psychological wage" of whiteness.

This bad story has proved remarkably resilient. It was what compelled poor Southern whites to fight and die in defense of slavery, an institution that crippled their own economic fortunes. It drove the atrocities of the Jim Crow laws, the domestic terrorism of groups such as the Ku Klux Klan, and the electoral ambitions of Dixiecrats and later the Republican Party, whose leaders adopted a Southern Strategy predicated on racial appeals to whites. Donald Trump tweaked his pitch to suit the era—swapping in illegal aliens and Muslims—but it was a familiar story, the one rich white Americans always tell less rich white Americans so that they'll blame their loss of status and security on people of color.

◆ ◆ ◆

As I struggled to make sense of the 2016 election, my mind kept spiraling back to one particular scene in American literature: Ahab, perched upon the quarterdeck of the Pequod, a "grand, ungodly, god-like man" with a prosthetic leg fashioned from a whale's jawbone. The captain has come to announce the true nature of his mission, which is not economic in nature but deeply personal. He seeks revenge against the leviathan that maimed him and exhorts his crew with a soliloquy Trumpian in pitch if not diction.

"All visible objects . . . are but pasteboard masks," Ahab roars. "If man will strike, strike through the mask! How can the prisoner reach outside except by thrusting through the wall? To me, the white whale is that wall, shoved near to me. Sometimes I think there's naught beyond. But 'tis enough. He tasks me; he heaps me; I see in him outrageous strength, with an inscrutable malice sinewing it. That inscrutable thing is chiefly what I hate; and be the white whale agent, or be the white whale principal, I will wreak that hate upon him. Talk not to me of blasphemy, man; I'd strike the sun if it insulted me."

It is this volcanic sense of grievance that fuels Melville's saga, that binds the crew of the Pequod—a coterie of races and temperaments, immigrants and exiles, one for each state of the union—to their leader. "Ahab's quenchless feud seemed mine," Ishmael tells us, rather helplessly. Who can blame the kid? Ahab is something like a natural force, a vortex of vindication as mighty as the beast he pursues. Not even the prophecies of his own mystical harpooner—who foresees the mission culminating in a hearse made of American wood—can moderate his impulses.

After four years of maniacal pursuit, Ahab spots his enemy and attacks. It does not go well. The wounded whale smites the Pequod, drowning all aboard and rendering the ship a hearse. In the end, "possessed by all the fallen angels," Ahab himself pierces the pale flank of his nemesis with his harpoon. But in the process, the rope winds up noosed around his neck and the beast drags him to his fate. Even a passing sky hawk gets snagged in the wreckage, "and so the bird of heaven, with archangelic shrieks, and his imperial beak thrust upwards, and his whole captive form folded in the flag of Ahab, went down with his ship, which, like Satan, would not sink to hell till she had dragged a living part of heaven along with her, and helmeted herself with it."

Melville is offering a mythic account of how one man's virile bombast can ensnare everyone and everything it encounters. The setting is nautical, the language epic, the allusions Biblical and Shakespearean. But the tale, stripped to its ribs, is about the seductive force of the wounded male ego, and how naturally a ship steered by men might tack to its vengeful course.

♦ ♦ ♦

The plot of *Moby Dick* pits man against the natural world. But its theme pits man against his own nature. The election of 2016 was, in its way, a retelling of this epic. Whether you choose to cast Trump as agent or principal hardly matters. What matters is that Americans joined the quest. Whether in rapture or disgust, we turned away from the compass of self-governance and toward the mesmerizing drama of aggression on display, the capitalist id unchained and all that it unchained within us. Trump struck through the mask. And it was enough.

When I started writing this book, in the months after the election, I was furious and frightened, worn down by decades of disappointment and determined, mostly, to launch harpoons at those I imagined to be my adversaries.

That, too, is a part of this story. The great peril of our age is not that we have turned into a nation of Ahabs, but of Ishmaels, passive observers too willing to embrace feuds that nourish our rancor and starve our common sense. It is this Manichean outlook that laid the groundwork for the ascent of Donald Trump and has, as of this writing, sustained his chaotic reign.

I am struggling in these pages to see Trumpism in a different light: as an opportunity to reckon with the bad stories at the heart of our great democratic experiment, and to recognize that often, embedded within these bad stories, are beautiful ideals and even correctives that might help us to contain the rage that has clouded our thoughts.

I have taken a patchwork approach to this project, one that knits statistical data, personal anecdote, cultural criticism, literary analysis, and, when called for, outright intellectual theft. I'm trying, in the broadest sense, to understand how the American story arrived at this point.

I've taken Ishmael as my guide here. For while it's true that he falls under the spell of Ahab's folly (as did I, as did I), he is also its only surviving witness and chronicler, the voice left to impart whatever wisdom might be dredged from the deep. Amid the spectacle of a mad captain and his murderous quarry, we mustn't forget that *Moby Dick* is a parable about our national destiny in which the only bulwark against self-inflicted tyranny is the telling of the story.

THE UNITED STATES IS
A REPRESENTATIVE DEMOCRACY

Several weeks before Election Day, when polls were suggesting Donald Trump was going to lose, perhaps quite badly, he began to insist that the American electoral system was rigged.

In the days and weeks after the election, those of us who had been most skeptical of this claim discovered that Trump had been right. Our system was so flagrantly rigged that a candidate could lose by nearly three million votes and still be declared the winner. He could lay claim to the most powerful office on Earth while enjoying the support of barely a quarter of all eligible voters. I have no intention of documenting the full extent of our electoral depravities; that would be another book. But it's worth a quick survey of the lowlights.

To begin, we must revisit the story of our Founding Fathers as a band of enlightened souls who sought equal representation in democracy. If that had been true, they would have forged a direct election system, in which every legal resident was entitled to one vote and the candidate with the most votes won.

That's never the way presidential elections in this country worked, because our democracy was forged in the colonies of the 18th century, the majority of which profited immensely by slavery. The Electoral College was a compromise that allowed Southern states to count slaves as part of their population, officially enfranchised at 60 percent, thanks to the Three-Fifths Clause. This is why four of the first five presidents were from Virginia, the state with the most people—if you count slaves.

The modern effects of this giveaway to our slave-owning founders have been profoundly undemocratic, and they travel far beyond subverting the popular will of the electorate. For instance, electoral votes are allegedly apportioned based on population. But all states, no matter how sparsely populated, are apportioned three, one for each senator and congressperson. As a result, a vote in Wyoming counts 3.5 times as much as a vote in New York or California. The effort to protect the interests of sparsely populated states led to a systemic bias against populous states.

Because electoral votes are winner-take-all in most states, modern candidates formulate policy for, and direct campaign efforts at, a small group of swing states, while virtually ignoring the rest. The result is a process that caters to a tiny segment of our population, and discourages non-swing state voters by making them feel that their votes won't matter.

Trump himself called the Electoral College "a disaster for a democracy" in 2012, after Obama defeated Mitt Romney. "We should have a revolution in this country! . . . The phoney [sic] electoral college made a laughing stock [sic] out of our nation. The loser one!"

Again, Trump was right. In 2016, the Electoral College amplified the power of rural areas, depressed turnout, stoked tribalism, and removed the central barrier to a candidacy predicated on broadly unpopular positions: winning the most votes.

◆ ◆ ◆

There were other stories that might have helped the public understand that Trump's path to 270 Electoral Votes wasn't as narrow as polls made it appear.

The most distressing of these was embedded within his talk of a rigged election. The basis for this claim, when he bothered to provide one, was a study indicating that our voting rolls included more than a million dead people, and that some voters were registered in two states. Given that Americans move and die, usually without informing the local election board, these facts should come as no surprise. Trump's insinuation was that some secret cabal stood ready to target these phantom voters and systematically perpetrate massive voter fraud on behalf of his opponent. But there are no election officials, of any political affiliation, who can point to more than a handful of isolated voter fraud cases.

So what were his ominous assertions really about? They are the newest incarnation of a hoary American tradition: voter suppression. In previous eras, these efforts took the form of Jim Crow laws that targeted people of color and the poor: poll taxes, literacy and property tests, selective purges of the voting rolls, and physical intimidation.

In 1965—a century after the Civil War—Congress passed the Voting Rights Act, which outlawed these discriminatory practices. Ever since, conservative politicians and activists have been trying to chip away at the law by promoting a false sense of crisis around voter fraud. Three years ago, they won their biggest battle to date: the Supreme Court ruled that states could pass restrictive voting laws without federal approval. Fourteen states did so, all with legislatures controlled by Republicans. These measures did not make voting impossible, merely more difficult, especially for the urban poor.

As intended, voting rates dipped in all these states by nearly two percent from 2012. On Election Day, new voter identification laws were enforced in Wisconsin and reduced turnout by 200,000 votes, in a state Clinton lost by 23,000. Milwaukee's poorest neighborhoods alone saw a drop of 41,000 votes.

In North Carolina, GOP lawmakers passed a voter ID law in 2013 that caused voter registration to plummet, before it was abolished in court for being racially discriminatory. Republicans then attempted to purge thousands from the state's voting rolls, which a federal judge deemed "insane." Another court noted that lawmakers had "requested data on the use, by race, of a number of voting practices" then crafted a law to disenfranchise African Americans.

GOP-controlled election boards also slashed early voting sites and reduced their hours in particular counties, especially on Sundays, when African-American churches sponsored "souls to the polls" voting drives. The result was that early voting turnout was 20 percent lower in so-called "suppressed counties" than in other counties. None of these tactics were a secret. The state GOP in North Carolina put out a press release before Election Day bragging that African-American turnout was down by 8.5 percent in early voting.

Oddly, there was almost no coverage of these efforts during the campaign. Instead, Trump's insinuations of voter fraud took center stage, diverting attention from verifiable voter suppression. This is what I have come to think of as *The Central Law of Bad Stories*. Bad stories don't just distort our belief system; they act to prevent more truthful stories from being heard.

◆ ◆ ◆

The proliferation of opinion polling had the perverse effect of suppressing the vote, as well. Here's how that worked. First, you had two historically unpopular candidates. Second, you had coverage that barely took note of the profound differences in their policies. Third, you had an unknown sum of citizens uninspired by Clinton but ready to vote against Trump. These marginal voters, confronted by an endless parade of surveys showing Clinton comfortably ahead in the final days of the race began to ask: Why should I bother to schlep to the polls on a Tuesday if she has it in the bag?

That was another factor almost nobody mentioned: presidential elections are held on *Tuesdays*. Why? Because of an 1845 law predicated on the notion that voting shouldn't interfere with the Sabbath, or with market day. See, farmers needed a day to drive their buggies to the county seat to vote, then a day to drive back . . . wait. Sabbath? Buggies? Is any of this relevant in 2016? No. Does it make any sense at all to hold our most important election on a workday? No. Does this further discourage turnout, especially among the working poor? Undoubtedly.

The reason the U.S. ranks 31 out of 35 in voter participation among advanced democracies—behind Slovakia, Greece, Mexico, and Turkey—is because our system of democracy has been rigged, structurally and logistically, by some combination of cynical partisan intent, class privilege, and abject negligence.

But the central reason 90 million Americans didn't exercise their franchise has more to do with psychological and emotional factors. On a fundamental level, people have to believe in the democratic process. That doesn't just require faith in the idea that *your* vote counts. It requires faith in the larger idea that *voting* matters, that who we elect at a local and state and federal level makes a difference in our lives. And it is here, at the level of basic disaffection, that American democracy faces its central crisis.

◆ ◆ ◆

I think here of the young woman who agreed to babysit our children on election night, a college senior who planned to apply to medical schools. Did she have any idea where the candidates stood on the issue of college tuition or student debt? Had she listened to any of the debates, at which Clinton raised these issues nine times? Did she know about Clinton's plan to make college debt-free and tuition free at public universities for families making less than $125,000?

Had she listened to Trump's response? "She can say all she wants about college tuition. And I'm a big proponent. We're going to do a lot of things for college tuition but the rest of the public is going to be paying for it."

Had it occurred to her that there was an obvious difference between how seriously these candidates were taking her life? Or that the outcome of the election might mean the difference between emerging from medical school with no debt or in hawk up to her eyeballs?

Before I could ask any of these questions, our sitter mentioned, rather sheepishly, that she was registered to vote in North Carolina but got mixed up about the absentee ballot deadline. She hadn't voted. That was her story. And it got more votes than either candidate.

OUR GRIEVANCES MATTER
MORE THAN OUR VULNERABILITIES

In a realpolitik overrun by bitter partisanship, civic apathy acts as a kind of dark matter: pervasive, invisible, and virtually impossible to quantify. It is, in essence, a form of privilege—the privilege of negligence—that arises in a population insulated from foreign threat and domestic hardship.

One of the most common electoral symptoms of this privilege is the so-called protest vote, in which citizens register their disgust for "the system" by voting for a candidate they know can't win. I make no excuses here for the ills of our modern two-party system, which amounts to a corrosive duopoly. I understand the desire to support the candidate who most closely aligns with your values.

But it's not idealism that motivates many protest voters. It's cynicism. Consider my friend Josh. He's a Harvard-educated computer scientist who works for a non-profit research institute funded, in part, by federal grants. His wife is a public school teacher and they have two daughters in middle school.

We don't talk much about politics, because Josh is one of those upbeat guys who considers the subject a bummer. From what I could discern, he supported John Kasich and viewed Trump as a joke. The last time I saw him before the election, he announced that he'd cast an early ballot for "the drunk and the stoner." He meant the Libertarian candidates, Gary Johnson and William Weld. Was he familiar with Johnson's policy positions? No, he told me. He voted for Johnson as a protest.

When I asked what that meant, he explained that the two-party system was broken and that Clinton would be a disaster because she'd be unable to get anything through Congress with the GOP in control of the House. I asked if voting for Johnson was, in a sense, endorsing the Republican strategy of intransigence, as well as gerrymandering, by penalizing Clinton for the actions of her opposition. He shrugged. We live in Massachusetts. What did it matter anyway?

◆ ◆ ◆

The next time I saw Josh, a few days after the election, a tense silence prevailed. We were driving to the gym near his work. Josh eventually confessed to being surprised by how upset his wife and daughters were after the election. I resisted the urge to point out the many reasons why that might be. Instead, I pressed him on one specific area of policy: climate change.

Josh argued that nobody knew yet what Trump would do.

"He called climate change a hoax," I said. "He promised to pull out of the Paris Accord. He's already begun stocking the Environmental Protection Agency with climate change deniers."

Josh offered no reply.

I took a deep breath. "Come on, man. You've dedicated your life to science. You know the risks of ignoring climate change. You've got two young daughters. This stuff should matter to you. If we're going to have a morally and intellectually serious discussion about the candidates, it has to be about their policies—"

"See, this is why your side lost!" Josh snapped. "That right there! That elite attitude! You're calling Trump supporters idiots. It's condescending."

"What are you talking about?" I said. "I didn't say a thing about Trump supporters. I'm talking to you."

In two decades of friendship, I'd never heard Josh speak so sharply. He was pissed at me for guilt tripping him. I was pissed at him for trivializing the election. But what struck me as we lapsed into another silence was the word he had used to convert his guilt into accusation: *elite*.

I'd never heard him use this word before, not even once. And yet it had leapt from his mouth reflexively, a little belch of punditry. *Elite* had become a kind of code word, one that right-wing politicians and pundits and even wealthy Harvard-educated scientists deployed to ward off the horrors of having to discuss policy. Anyone who wanted to talk about that stuff was being *elite* and being *elite* meant you were talking down to someone.

Trump used the word to condemn anyone or anything too serious, from the *New York Times* to President Obama to climate scientists. In this sense, *elite* served the same basic function as *politically correct*, the term he used to bludgeon any sustained consideration of bigotry. They were deployed not just to dodge a particular discussion, but to recast cynicism as a form of wisdom, and moral negligence as a form of martyrdom.

◆ ◆ ◆

Josh is maybe the nicest guy I know. He felt bad for snapping at me. Maybe, to some extent, he felt bad for his vote. Whatever the reason, toward the end of our drive, he confessed to something I'd never known about him. After the financial crisis of 2008, he had been fired abruptly from a previous job and remained unemployed for several months. His daughters were toddlers, his wife had quit her job, and he was just a few years into a mortgage on a new home. During this period—which I remembered as deeply anguishing for Josh—Obama's stimulus package had footed most of the bill for his family's medical insurance.

What Josh did not mention was that every Republican in the House had voted against the American Recovery and Reinvestment Act. If the GOP had had the votes, they would have blocked the stimulus altogether, leaving Josh with a nasty choice: pay thousands for health insurance or lose coverage.

Yet Josh felt no particular gratitude toward Obama, or the Democrats who had fought for the law. Nor did he feel any impetus to acquaint himself with the wildly divergent policy positions of the 2016 presidential candidates. Less than seven years since the stimulus saved his bacon, his faith in the government's capacity to aid and comfort families like his own had completely evaporated.

Josh took his grievances seriously but not his vulnerabilities.

◆ ◆ ◆

In a sense, Trumpism was the inevitable outgrowth of this mentality. Traditional politicians attempt to win support by selling a legislative program that will produce specific benefits: jobs or tax cuts or ideologically desirable judicial appointments. Trump was only nominally interested in such results. His central argument was that politics—the smug pieties, the arcane rules, the gentle norms—was bullshit. In other words, he was a protest candidate. Many of those who

voted for him were voting against their own curdled perceptions of government.

A few days after the election, for instance, I found myself
engaged in a brief conversation with a well-heeled neighbor.
She couldn't understand why everyone was so freaked out.
"The Obamas never really did anything for me," she said.
"They never looked out for the middle class. They helped
the poor, the rich took care of themselves, but my daughter
didn't get any help with college. And when my parents died
there was barely anything left."

I didn't know what to make of these complaints. Was she
angry about the estate tax, a measure that applied only to
inheritances that exceeded five million dollars? Did she expect Obama to defray the tuition at the private college her
daughter attended?

"And why didn't Obama visit Israel?" she continued. "He
didn't go there once during his whole time in office. What
does that say?"

I had a distinct memory that Obama *had* gone to Israel—
in fact, he visited twice—but I kept my mouth shut. I was in
that peculiar psychic space, now so common in our republic,
where one senses not just a divergence of political belief but
the impossibility of coherent discourse.

What was this woman really saying in the end? She was
saying that Obama had failed to honor a bargain whose
terms she, as a citizen, felt free to shift according to her whim.
It was an argument of such subjective force, and ingrained

entitlement, as to be impervious. At the same time, she was being utterly sincere. This was what democracy *felt* like to her.

She saw no relationship between her life and the election beyond the lazy hope that the new guy would give her more stuff than the last. She felt no need to evaluate the veracity of the claims made by or about either candidate, the policies they proposed, or the likely consequences of these policies. This negligence didn't make her exceptional. It made her typical.

◆ ◆ ◆

My brother-in-law explained to me that Obama's presidency hadn't affected him because he works for FedEx, which offers private health insurance. He appeared unaware that the Affordable Care Act required employers to provide numerous essential benefits such as preventive care. Nor had he thought much about what his life would have been like if the Obama administration had not pursued policies—in the face of vehement opposition—that resuscitated the banking sector and the housing market, that his company would have been one of the first hit, that he might have lost his job, that he never would have been able to build his new home. My brother-in-law is a smart guy who had somehow come to believe that only people insured under Obamacare had a stake in his presidency.

And what of Obamacare recipients? Debbie Mills, a small business owner in the town of Corbin, Kentucky, told a reporter from Vox.com that she stopped buying private health insurance more than a decade ago, because the premiums had become too expensive. When Obamacare became available in her state, she signed up and received a huge tax credit, which allowed her to pay $115 monthly for a plan that covered her, her husband, and her teenage son. This insurance became life saving in 2016, when her husband went on the waiting list for a liver transplant.

Over the course of the campaign, Trump pledged to repeal Obamacare daily. Mills knew this would have devastating consequences for her family. She voted for him anyway. She said she was drawn to Trump because he was a straight-talking businessman who would shake up Washington and bring jobs to her town. She simply chose not to acknowledge his straight talk about killing Obamacare.

After the election, the Vox reporter visited Mills. Their interview quickly turned into a kind of therapy session, with the reporter having to reassure Mills that she and her sick husband wouldn't be kicked off their insurance—at least not immediately. "You're scaring me now," Mills said. "I'm afraid now that the insurance is going to go away and we're going to be up a creek."

It would be easy to accuse Mills of being a sucker, or any of the other imprecations elitists love to lob. A gentler diagnosis is that she represents our national habit of taking our grievances seriously but not our vulnerabilities.

ECONOMIC ANGUISH
FUELED TRUMPISM

On the eve of the 2016 Democratic National Convention, I flew out to Ohio to meet with writing students at Ashland University. Ashland is a city of 20,000 that serves as the seat to a rural county of the same name. It sits halfway between Cleveland and Columbus, just off Interstate 71.

As a political junkie residing in Massachusetts, I was elated to visit an actual swing state in the thick of an actual election year. I marched around asking everybody I met about the race. The university folk all insisted Trump was too crazy to win. The cashier at the discount market where I loaded up on snacks insisted Clinton would be indicted before Election Day. The undergraduate who drove me around town, a native of Ashland County, sounded uncertain. She said most of her kin were going to vote for Trump but she couldn't be sure because they had stopped talking politics with her after she enrolled in college.

I had arrived in Ohio with my own preconceived notions, of course, shaped by the many stories I'd read about the growing disenchantment of working-class voters over the loss of manufacturing. Ashland fit the profile. The biggest factory in town, which once employed 1,100 workers making pipes and haying tools, was long gone. The second largest had shipped hundreds of jobs to China a decade ago. The city still had a college, some small businesses, and acres of service industry jobs: chain hotels, fast food joints, a vast Walmart filled with cheap foreign goods, which rose from an ocean of asphalt that girdled the highway. The terrain around Ashland had changed, too, as small crop farms gave way to large-scale dairy and livestock operations.

I remember telling my wife on the last day of my visit that a Trump presidency didn't feel so far-fetched out here in Ashland. On election night, as Trump racked up gaudy margins in the rural enclaves of the Midwest, I thought of Ashland. The county went for McCain by 5,800 votes in 2008, and Romney by 7,000 votes four years later. Trump beat Clinton by 11,500.

◆ ◆ ◆

This story was the one most widely circulated in the days after the election, often bolstered by a prescient quote from the 1998 book *Achieving Our Country* by the late philosopher

Richard Rorty. Rorty argued that the American left made a grave moral and strategic error when it shifted focus from economic injustice to identity politics. He prophesized that unskilled workers, left in the lurch, would eventually "decide that the system has failed and start looking around for a strongman to vote for," a jocular bigot able to channel their resentment "about having their manners dictated to them by college graduates."

Media commentators, liberal ones especially, gravitated to Rorty's theory because it presented Trumpism as a rational, if disturbing, response to economic frustrations, which progressive policy could presumably fix.

But the more social scientists crunched the election data, the less sense it made. The majority of Trump voters, for instance, were middle-class and wealthy suburbanites. More significantly, Trump crushed Clinton in counties where unemployment had fallen in recent years. The jobless rate in Ashland County stood at 14.7 percent in 2010. By the time I visited, it had shrunk to 4.3 percent.

Am I saying that Rorty was wrong? No. He was spot-on in foreseeing how a sense of futility and anti-elitist rage would ripple through the realpolitik. (Recall the young college student who drove me around in Ashland, the one whose relatives wouldn't talk politics with her.) But Rorty was telling only a small part of a much larger story, one in which Trump is no more than an unexpected coda.

After all, he's been trotting out the same pitch for three decades. His first speech as a presidential aspirant, delivered in 1987, featured all his standard complaints: America was a disaster. We were being kicked around. The world was laughing at us. Why? Because of foreigners and politicians and eggheads and softies. "If the right man doesn't get into office you're going to see a catastrophe in this country like you're never going to believe," he huffed. "And then you'll be begging for the right man." To understand how Trump went from a fringe character to the right man, we have to understand how the psychology and attitudes of the electorate shifted around him.

That begins with the rise of polarization.

◆ ◆ ◆

It can be easy to lose sight of this, but there was a time in American politics when the central motivation was pride in one's own party. In the 1950s, only 10 percent of voters had negative feelings toward the opposing party. That number now stands at 90 percent. Those who hold "very unfavorable" views of the other party have tripled since 1994. The result is that negative partisanship has become the default setting of our electorate, a culturally sanctioned form of discrimination.

In 1960, only one in twenty Americans voiced an objection to a child marrying a member of the opposing party.

As of 2010, the figure stood at half of all Republicans, and a third of Democrats.

What's more perplexing is *why* partisanship has spiked so dramatically. Because political identity is voluntary, people treat it as fair game for hatred in a way they never would with race or gender. Political scientists such as Alan Abramowitz and Steven Webster see the rise in negative partisanship as "part of a vicious cycle of mutually reinforcing elite and mass behavior." They mean that voters and politicians are egging each other on.

A 2014 study of political attitudes conducted by political scientists at Stanford and Princeton is more pointed. "Our evidence demonstrates that hostile feelings for the opposing party are ingrained," they concluded, "to a degree that exceeds discrimination based on race. We note that the willingness of partisans to display open animus for opposing partisans can be attributed to the absence of norms governing the expression of negative sentiment and that increased partisan affect provides an incentive for elites to engage in confrontation rather than cooperation." Not only is political bigotry now more powerful than racial bigotry, but it's us voters who drive the cycle of animus.

It's too easy to blame hyper-partisan politicians or media outlets. They are merely symptoms of a growing prejudice that resides within us.

◆ ◆ ◆

In the fall of 2016, I taught a course in literary journalism at Wesleyan. A month before the election, I had my class read an in-depth profile of a fanatical Trump supporter in the *Washington Post*. Using this as a model, I asked my students to interview a person whose political views were in direct opposition to their own. Only two students completed the assignment. The rest claimed they couldn't track down such a person.

The atmosphere in class after the election was bereft. We were into the workshop phase by then and one student submitted an essay denouncing Trump. The piece made no effort to divine the motives of the 62 million Americans who had voted for him, beyond imputing their hatred. In class, I gently suggested that empathy might lead him to a more nuanced set of explanations.

"I don't have any empathy for Trump voters," the author replied.

He didn't mean that he couldn't summon any empathy. He meant that it would be a betrayal of his principles to try. Several of his classmates nodded.

I found this statement distressing as a teacher. The central point of a class on literary journalism, so far as I had conceived it, was to compel students to recognize that there was a big, complex world outside of their experience, and that the most useful attitude to adopt toward this world was not one of contempt but humble curiosity. I understood my student's desire to condemn the outcome of the election. But bad outcomes, as I had labored to convey, were the result of bad stories. It was the duty of journalists to listen to these stories. Then to use the tools at their disposal—reporting, research, reflection—to interrogate them, to determine the ways in which they were shaped by rage and confusion and disappointment rather than, say, facts or logic or compassion.

All semester long, I'd argued that the whole point of literature, and by extension literary journalism, is to complicate our own moral perceptions by forcing us to accept that other people matter, that their struggles and hardships matter, and that their delusions cannot be tamed until they are understood. Propaganda has the opposite aim: to simplify moral action by dismissing the humanity of others.

I tell this story—before turning my attention to Trump voters—to emphasize that polarized thinking afflicts *all of us*. To those moderate or liberal readers old enough, I invite you to conduct a thought experiment. Try to recall what it was like to spot a Bob Dole bumper sticker on someone's car. Think about what sort of judgments you made about the driver. Now think about the judgments you made about the driver when you saw a Trump bumper sticker. Here's my list: white, male, racist, misogynist, uneducated, gun-owning, gullible, and paranoid.

This sort of bigotry is what I have in common with my student.

◆ ◆ ◆

As a reminder: reflexive partisan hostility is not the result of gridlock, but its cause. Republicans in Congress made obstructing Obama their central agenda because any talk of compromise would be met with the threat of a primary challenge from someone more suitably unyielding. This is why the GOP is captive to its most extreme partisans, and why Trump's path to the nomination was not just predictable, but inevitable.

He intuitively exploited "the absence of norms governing the expression of negative sentiment." For years, GOP leaders issued various dog whistles. Trump wolf whistled his prejudice and his poll numbers surged.

Party officials, pollsters, and the media viewed his bombast as a sure sign of doom in the general election. But they had underestimated the magnetic power of negative partisanship. Threatening to jail his opponent or invoking a fantasy of her assassination was no longer going too far.

Exit polls showed that 90 percent of Republicans came home to Trump. They voted for him even if they disagreed with his core positions on immigration and trade. Twenty-seven percent of whites voted for him even though they wanted the next president to have more liberal policies. Nearly a quarter of Trump voters said he lacked the temperament to be president, and was not qualified for the office. Seventeen percent said they were "scared" or "concerned" about a President Trump.

That sounds puzzling until you consider the percentage of Trump voters who reported being scared or concerned about a Clinton presidency: 94.

◆ ◆ ◆

None of this should have come as a complete surprise, given the warning the historian Richard Hofstadter issued 50 years ago, in his seminal tract *The Paranoid Style in American Politics*. "American politics has often been an arena for angry minds," he observed. "In recent years we have seen angry minds at work mainly among extreme right-wingers, who have now demonstrated . . . how much political leverage can be got out of the animosities and passions of a small minority. But behind this I believe there is a style of mind that is far from new and that is not necessarily right-wing. I call it the paranoid style simply because no other word adequately evokes the sense of heated exaggeration, suspiciousness, and conspiratorial fantasy that I have in mind."

Trump undoubtedly leveraged the "animosities and passions of a small minority" to win the GOP nomination. But he was never some reality TV revolutionary. Trump was the new face of an old political tradition, one that stretches from the redbaiting inquisition of Joseph McCarthy to the zealots who inveighed against the international gold ring at the turn of the 19th century.

Over the past few decades, the GOP has revived this paranoid style, turning legislative programs into pogroms. Obama's effort to expand medical coverage became "a government takeover of health care." Universal background checks on firearms sales became a prelude to wide-scale gun seizures. Trump simply shoved this conspiratorial mindset onto the brightest stage in American politics.

Here's how Trump put it in his 2007 book, *Think Big*: "The world is a vicious and brutal place. We think we're civilized. In truth, it's a cruel world and people are ruthless. They act nice to your face, but underneath they're out to kill you . . . Even your friends are out to get you." Such ideation breeds militancy. Social conflict is not "something to be mediated and compromised," Hofstadter notes. Instead, the paranoid exhorts his followers to "fight things out to the finish," which should explain the pleasure Trump took in seeing protestors roughed up at his rallies.

"The paranoid spokesman sees the fate of conspiracy in apocalyptic terms," is how Hofstadter put it. "He is always manning the barricades of civilization."

◆ ◆ ◆

The story Trump told about America was of a holy land infiltrated by foreigners who lurked beyond, and within, our borders. Whites unsettled by a rising demographic tide flocked to his rallies to partake in a grand drama of national reclamation whose central feature was an orgiastic denunciation of those dark, and dark-skinned, forces aligned against their cause.

This style of nationalism—familiar to anyone versed in the Old Testament—has been on the rise for decades in Europe. Just like here, most observers assumed these movements were driven by economic anxiety stemming from globalization. But political scientists at Harvard and the University of Michigan who tracked social survey data from nearly 300,000 Europeans over a dozen years discovered, to their astonishment, that the factors predicting support for nationalists weren't economic at all, but social, racial, and attitudinal.

True believers weren't wage slaves pining for better jobs. They were self-employed, or small business owners—the petty bourgeoisie, basically—who wanted white privilege preserved and laws enforced and immigrants deported. Demographically, this far-right coalition was "concentrated among the older generation, men, the religious, majority populations, and the less educated—sectors generally left behind by progressive tides of cultural value change."

That's a pretty sharp thumbnail of the Trump base. And it helps explain why his base embraced proposals that were, to put it gently, regressive. In South Carolina, for instance, 75 percent of all Republicans favored banning Muslims from America. A third of Trump partisans wanted to ban gays and lesbians; twenty percent felt Lincoln shouldn't have freed the slaves.

More moderate Trump supporters inevitably downplay these stats. But research compiled by the political scientist Philip Klinkner shows that racial resentment was second only to party identification as a driver of Trump support. As you move from the least to the most resentful view of African Americans, support for Trump climbs 44 points. Klinkner assumed factors such as income and economic pessimism would also predict Trump support. They did not. As with European far-right movements, economic stress wasn't triggering racial resentment. It was already there, a cause in search of a candidate.

Even more depressing was a survey given to 2,000 white Americans that detected "substantial levels of dehumanization among Trump supporters" across all income levels. More than half thought African Americans were less evolved. Twenty-seven percent described them as "lacking self-restraint, like animals."

Reading this description sent me reeling back to one of the enduring images from the campaign trail: the elderly

white man who sucker-punched an African-American pro-
tester in the face as police were escorting him out of a Trump
rally in North Carolina. The victim of this assault was immediately detained by police officers. The perpetrator, John
McGraw, was neither detained nor arrested at the event. He
was, however, interviewed by a TV crew.

"You bet I liked it," he said of the rally. What was his favor-
ite part? "Knocking the hell out of that big mouth. We don't
know who he is, but we know he's not acting like an American.
The next time we see him, we might have to kill him."

◆ ◆ ◆

I thought, too, about an old Ray Bradbury short story entitled
"And the Rock Cried Out." It begins with a pair of wealthy
white Americans, John and Leonora Webb, on vacation in
a small Latin American country. The year is 1963. A great
war has killed most of the population of the United States,
Europe, and Russia. "The day of the white people of the earth
is over and finished," a newspaper announces.

What ensues is a series of excruciating scenes in which
the Webbs are stripped of their possessions and hunted down
by natives. The couple finds safe harbor at a hotel with a manager who offers them a chance to save themselves, if they're
willing to accept menial work in the kitchen. But the Webbs
have lived within their privilege for so long they can't envision a life without it. They refuse.

"We have never let ourselves think about our being a minority," Webb tells his wife, "and now it's hard to get used to the fact."

"We're being consistent, anyway," she replies, as they march stoically toward death. "Spoiled, but consistent."

The story—which Bradbury composed in 1953, at the height of American imperial power—is a grisly parable in which the Webbs become a blood sacrifice for centuries of racial and economic hegemony. It kept coming to mind because it taps into a primal fear that lives inside men like John McGraw: that they are destined to become prey. No one ever says this out loud. But for a large segment of the American population (much larger than anyone realized) the specter of racial revenge feels more urgent than threats such as climate change or nuclear winter. This was the dystopia that Trump consistently plugged into: Fear of a Brown Planet.

It's the reason he continually portrayed minorities as predatory, from Mexican rapists to African-American cop killers to Muslim sleeper cells. It's the reason his fairytales about Muslims cheering as the Twin Towers fell, and his bogus stats about black-on-white crime, held such power. White supremacists understood Trump instantly and intuitively, because racial anxiety animates their worldview. The rest of us never quite grasped how persuasive this appeal was.

We should have.

◆ ◆ ◆

In April of 1989, a white woman jogging through Central Park was raped and severely assaulted. That same night, a large group of boys entered the park from East Harlem. Some threw rocks at cars, others assaulted and robbed passersby. The police took a number into custody and quickly developed a theory that five of them (the Central Park Five) had committed the rape. The suspects, four African Americans and one Hispanic, confessed after lengthy police interrogations. The press seized on the brutality of the crime, and its racial dynamics, to fan hysteria among New Yorkers. They created a parable suited to the roiling anxieties of a city in which both violent crime and income inequality had spiked, in which crack ravaged poor neighborhoods while Wall Street minted millionaires.

Two weeks after the arrests, Donald Trump took out full-page ads in the city's four major dailies, topped by two giant headlines:

BRING BACK THE DEATH PENALTY.

BRING BACK OUR POLICE!

A Trump polemic ensued:

What has happened to our city over the past ten years? What has happened to law and order ... What has happened to the respect for authority? What has happened is the complete breakdown of life as we knew it. . . . Mayor Koch has stated that hate and rancor should be removed from our hearts. I do not think so. I want to hate these muggers and murderers. They should be forced to suffer and, when they kill, they should be executed for their crimes . . . I am not looking to psychoanalyze or understand them. I am looking to punish them.

Criminals must be told that their CIVIL LIBERTIES END WHEN AN ATTACK ON OUR SAFETY BEGINS!

The effect of these ads was immediate. One woman suggested, on live television, that the suspects be castrated. Pat Buchanan, a former White House advisor who later outmaneuvered Trump for the Reform Party's presidential nomination, called for them to be hanged in Central Park by June 1. As a reminder: they had yet to be tried.

Trump's civic impulses hadn't been awakened by crime as it affected all New Yorkers. After all, there were thousands of rapes in New York City in 1989, including one the same day as the Central Park case in which an African-American woman was thrown off a four-story building in Brooklyn. What mattered to Trump, what occasioned his outrage, was the story of dark-skinned thugs invading an iconic Manhattan preserve to defile a white female investment banker.

It's worth noting the historical roots of a story like this, which stretch back to the era that gave Manhattan its name. The British who settled New England were absolutely petrified of Native Americans. It was this terror that helped spark the Salem Witch Trials and later justified the wholesale slaughter of natives. White colonists were haunted, too, by the possibility that slaves would rise up and exact a revenge commensurate with the barbarism of their subjugation. Courage and valor have been central virtues in the American psyche precisely because we are a population steeped in the fear Bradbury identified: an uprising of the dark other.

◆ ◆ ◆

Although no physical evidence linked them to the crime, the Central Park Five were convicted on the basis of their police confessions. In 2002, a judge vacated the guilty verdicts, after DNA evidence exonerated them, and identified the actual perpetrator, a serial rapist who confessed to the crime and provided prosecutors precise details of how he carried it out. The Central Park Five was a bad story that led to a bad outcome.

Trump refused to accept the exoneration and scoffed at the notion that he should apologize. He condemned the city's 2014 decision to compensate the five men for their suffering.

"I think people are tired of politically correct. I just attacked the Central Park Five settlement. Who's going to do that?"

Many of us look at a statement like that as heartless. But within the American electorate there is a certain kind of voter who cares more about social order than due process. They are said to have an *authoritarian mindset*. This doesn't mean they support authoritarian regimes. It's a psychological profile, not a political label. Voters with the authoritarian mindset value discipline and stability, and fear outsiders, especially those who portend change. When they feel threatened, they look to leaders who offer strong, simple, punitive solutions—even and especially if these solutions violate previously accepted moral norms.

In the fall of 2016, a PhD student named Matthew MacWilliams, who studies authoritarianism, began to suspect Trump supporters fell into this category. He polled likely voters and found that the authoritarian mindset predicted support for Trump more reliably than any other indicator, including racial and economic factors.

Think again about Trump's Central Park Five ad, the one calling for them to be executed. To people with an authoritarian mindset this kind of rhetoric is thrilling precisely because it flouts the rules that handcuff weaker leaders. Right from the beginning, Trump defined America as a nation under siege and nominated himself as the only guy strong enough to solve the crises that had overrun the weaklings in Washington. Without exception, these solutions were strong, simple, and punitive. Mexican rapists? *Build a wall.* Illegal immigrants? *Deportation squad.* Terrorists? *Kill their families.* Captured terrorists? *Torture.* Muslim Americans? *National registry.* Chinese? *Trade war.* Disruptive protestors? *Assault them.*

He lavished praise on authoritarians for being strong leaders. One of the most alarming reports during the campaign came from a foreign policy expert who advised Trump and claimed that the candidate had asked, three times, why, if the U.S. had nuclear weapons, it couldn't use them.

♦ ♦ ♦

GOP leaders often reacted with horror to these revelations. But the party had been catering to the authoritarian mindset for the past half century.

Much has been made, for instance, of Nixon's Southern Strategy of 1968. The accepted wisdom is that Nixon converted white Dixiecrats into Republicans by hustling racial resentment. But he was making a broader appeal to his Silent Majority, one that echoed the paranoia Goldwater had mainstreamed four years earlier. America had gone berserk. Race riots plagued its cities; violence beset its college campuses. The time had come for a candidate who would restore order before it was too late.

This appeal was somewhat obscured during the Reagan Revolution, because Reagan had the Soviet Union, a truly authoritarian regime, as his foil. During the George W. Bush era, Americans defined themselves in opposition to Islamic fundamentalism. But the underlying message of the party—beyond tax cuts and deregulation, the goodies forever pledged to its donor class—was a promise to crack down on anyone who broached traditional values. This has meant opposing social change in any form: civil rights legislation, hippie agitators, women's rights, gay rights, criminal justice reform, environmentalism, and, more recently, globalization and immigration.

Trump creamed a field of traditional conservatives in the 2016 primaries because he emerged as a fiery spokesman for racial and authoritarian appeals that party leaders had more quietly embraced as an electoral asset. Once he was the nominee, the power of negative partisanship kept him competitive.

TRUMP WAS A CHANGE AGENT

These underlying dynamics help expose a set of interrelated bad stories we heard constantly over the course of the campaign.

The first was that Trump needed to *pivot* away from his extreme rhetoric to a more acceptable form of economic populism. When was he going to pivot? Could his advisors get him to pivot? He'll lose if he doesn't pivot soon! In fact, he won because he *didn't* pivot. He refused to abandon the most virulent aspects of his rhetoric, and this defiance reinforced his disruptive mystique.

What marked Trump as disruptive was his attitude, not his ideas. He repudiated "politics as usual" by importing a brand of impulsive emotionalism into a milieu loathed for its cautious calculation. He refused to disavow or apologize for offensive statements. He reacted to slights with a defensive rancor most of us recognized from our own lives.

It's important to acknowledge this psychic identification, because it helps explain why Trump proved such an alluring figure, not only to his loyalists but to his critics. To those of us deeply invested in the story of our own virtue, Trump served as public vexation and secret vice. It was exciting to watch a human being so completely liberated from the restraints of a functioning conscience. We woke up each morning itching to open our browsers. And Trump rewarded our devotion by continually generating new affronts to our decency. He was the tireless adolescent forever trolling the unsecured border of our adulthood. We watched and listened and clicked and posted and tweeted and did so with such urgency that we lost sight, rather quickly, of the dull fact that elections are supposed to be about policies.

◆ ◆ ◆

Trump was an *unpredictable character*. That was the notion frantically promoted by both the campaigns and faithfully aped by most of the media. It was another bad story. In fact, Trump may be the most predictable character ever to arise in our public life.

To understand what I mean here, it's useful to consider the two basic types of literary characters E.M. Forster defines in *Aspects of the Novel*. Round characters are those who confront the dangers of self-revelation and change as a result. Flat characters remain static, incapable of change.

This does not mean that flat characters are incapable of taking action. On the contrary, they are very good at taking action because they are uninhibited by self-reflection. They often drive plots. Achilles, Iago, Kurtz, and (of course) Ahab are supreme examples of the genus. But to call these characters unpredictable is to confuse outcome with motive, instinct with intellection. They are unpredictable only in the narrow sense that an enraged bull is unpredictable.

There were moments during the campaign when I felt an acute sense of just how tiresome Trump was. He was capable of pivoting, but only between two poles of action: the pursuit of adulation and the desecration of his critics. Those were literally his only two dance moves. He displayed no sense of wonder or curiosity, no capacity to experience the emotions most closely associated with the soul: doubt, sorrow, mercy. He lived instead within a fortress of defensive emotions erected to guard against any hint of vulnerability. This was the source of his resilience.

Because it turns out that human beings are constantly constructing two stories about themselves. The first is the story of how we want the world to view us, the polished act we perform in public. The second is the story of who we know ourselves to be, the secret script of forbidden thoughts and feelings we tuck under the pillow of our privacy. Voters had a visceral response to Trump because he told that second story without shame. He was, in some sense, a kind of superhero, a man with no subtext or subconscious, all raw need and glaring projection.

I'm not suggesting that Trump, the human being, is a soulless monster. On the contrary, any person so desperate to convey strength is obviously contending with an inner life plagued by weakness. My own hunch is that Trump never experienced a sense of being unconditionally loved, what psychologists call *attachment*. The best he could hope for within his family of origin was to please his domineering father through aggression. Because he never developed an intrinsic sense of self-worth, he can't protect himself from feelings of inadequacy. I'm not defending Trump here, only noting that whatever we might wish to call evil within his character stems from a distortion of love. This is why Trump proved especially captivating to disaffected Americans. He embodied the fantasy that our most primal terrors—of losing status, of being unworthy of love or left behind—could be converted into omnipotence.

His campaign aimed squarely at psychic wounds too painful to be acknowledged and therefore impervious to rational discourse. Every time some pundit mocked the candidate or his supporters, or lectured them, or even asked them questions in a sober tone of voice, they were merely pouring more rocket fuel into the Trump Express.

◆ ◆ ◆

It was difficult, watching Trump bluff his way through the debates, not to think of Mencken: "As democracy is perfected, the office of president represents, more and more closely, the inner soul of the people. On some great and glorious day the plain folks of the land will reach their heart's desire at last and the White House will be adorned by a downright moron."

What reverberates here is the first sentence. Trump represented, and was therefore able to exploit, crucial aspects of the national character: our intellectual incuriosity, our hunger for distraction, a credulousness arising from our immersion in the razzle dazzle of marketing. He sold himself as a populist not by adopting populist policies but denouncing elitists. His tax plan funneled billions to the economic elite but nobody bothered to read the fine print. He successfully spun his political inexperience as purity because of our own fevered mistrust of government. His boasts that he knew better than career politicians mirrored our own arrogance. Consider the 2015 Pew Survey in which 55 percent of the respondents claimed "ordinary Americans" would do a better job than elected officials.

Trump embodied the duality at the heart of this nation's cult of success. Objectively, he tanked everything he touched: casinos, airlines, marriages, football teams, fake universities. But he reacted to these flops by defiantly—almost poignantly—declaring victory. He became the con artist lurking within all of us, the Facebook self-promoter and resume padder writ large. Each scam produced a new ledger of debts and lawsuits. But Trump skimmed his take and kept moving. He became the miraculous bearer of a fragile capitalist fairytale, the one in which impregnable self-belief is enough to spin disgrace into gold.

The election became, in many ways, a moratorium on the state of the American soul. Clinton went with cautious preparedness. Trump bet on profane bluster, understanding that an unholy crusader stood at least a puncher's chance against a holier-than-thou politician.

◆ ◆ ◆

None of this—the rise of an outsider populist, the psychic triumph of personality over policy—is especially new. Consider this dispatch from the campaign trail: "He gets enormous crowds wherever he goes . . . He has caught on as a personality even if his policies have not. It is common to hear, 'OK, so a lot of his ideas are cockeyed, but at least he tells you where he stands. He isn't afraid to speak up, the way others are.'" This is Gore Vidal writing, in 1964, about the dark horse GOP nominee Barry Goldwater.

This brings us to a second bad story, the one about how Trump was going to shake up Washington. Media outlets provided breathless coverage of his brazen statements and his violent rallies. They marveled at his repudiation of political tradition and ritual. But they largely ignored the reactionary nature of his policies. He provided the spectacle of disruption, for which he was magically accredited with the reputation of a change agent.

If you were properly attuned, you could hear him working this angle during the debates, in which he deftly hung the mantle of the status quo on Clinton: *She's been in politics for the last 30 years. She never gets anything done.*

Clinton won the debates, but she never attacked the fallacy at the heart of his campaign. Neither she, nor our Fourth Estate, ever forced him to explain how his policies—tax cuts for the rich, deregulation, scapegoating people of color—qualified him as a change agent. Every single proposal he made echoed back to some mythic past in which American prestige would be restored, our factories and mines would boom again, our streets would be made safe, women would know their place, and globalization would magically disappear, along with climate change, feminism, and other modern abominations.

The Trump agenda was about *resisting* change at all costs.

◆ ◆ ◆

The musician and poet Gil Scott-Heron diagnosed the situation years ago, when another entertainer ascended to the presidency:

The idea concerns the fact that this country wants nostalgia. They want to go back as far as they can—even if it's only as far as last week. Not to face now or tomorrow, but to face backwards. And yesterday was the day of our cinema heroes riding to the rescue at the last possible moment. The day of the man in the white hat or the man on the white horse . . . someone always came to save America at the last moment—especially in "B" movies. And when America found itself having a hard time facing the future, they looked for people like John Wayne. But since John Wayne was no longer available, they settled for Ronald Reagan and it has placed us in a situation that we can only look at like a "B" movie.

Scott-Heron was writing about a political regression he assumed had reached its zenith with the star of *Bedtime for Bonzo* napping in the Oval Office. But he had underestimated the forces aligned against the evolution of American democracy. It might be said that, in 2016, when Americans found themselves having a hard time facing the future, they looked for people like Ronald Reagan. Because Ronald Reagan was no longer available, they settled for Donald Trump.

◆ ◆ ◆

At this point, biographers and journalists have done a thorough rototill on Trump's childhood. We know that he worshipped his dad, who owned a bunch of low-income buildings in Queens. We know Fred Trump was arrested at a Klan rally as a younger man, that he didn't like renting apartments to African Americans, that he was sued by the federal government for discriminatory housing practices and forced to desegregate his properties. We know he used to take young Donald around with him to collect rents, and later employed him in the family business. We know that he urged his son to be "a killer" and shipped him off to a military boarding school at age twelve.

We know that Trump, as a budding real estate magnate, sought out as his mentors Roy Cohn, the menacing lawyer who served as Joseph McCarthy's attack dog, and Roger Stone, a Nixon-era dirty trickster, who reinforced his father's creed. Trump came to see life as "a series of battles" in which threats, insults, and deception helped you win. His upbringing and his moral training represent a hothouse for the authoritarian mindset. When he told New Yorkers, "maybe hate is what we need if we're gonna get something done," he meant it.

Although born into affluence, Trump developed a worldview indifferent, or perhaps hostile, to noblesse oblige—the notion, exemplified by the Kennedys, that nobility extends beyond lineage and requires compassion for the less fortunate. From early on, Trump favored a *social dominance orientation*, which describes the sort of person hung up on creating a hierarchy so he can be at the top of it. Narcissistic Darwinism (a term I believe I just invented) might also apply.

It sounds like a pretty miserable way to live, frankly, which is why Trump's aggression has always struck me as a shoddy disguise for despair. For all the glitz and frolicking of his professional life—casinos, pageants, TV shows—he never seems happy. When he spoke on the campaign trail about how much fun his rallies were, he was referring, more often than not, to the abuse inflicted on protesters or reporters.

So much of his behavior registers as cruel, even sociopathic. But what I often sense is something closer to the abject: a young child who never experienced tenderness, who was told to be a killer rather than a little boy, who never internalized any sense of forgiveness and is therefore unable to forgive the world around him.

WHAT AMUSES US CAN'T HURT US

At the risk of outing myself as a science fiction geek, let me return for a moment to Bradbury, and his 1953 classic *Fahrenheit 451*. The book is generally misunderstood as a tale about censorship. Bradbury's central concern wasn't the tyranny of the State, though. It was the self-induced triviality of the people. The scene most vital to understanding the novel is triggered not by a book burning but a failed book group.

Guy Montag, a fireman charged with burning the possessions of those caught reading, secretly becomes fascinated by books. One night he returns home and finds his wife Mildred and her friends sitting before the Parlor Walls, huge screens that provide insipid, around-the-clock entertainment. He unplugs the Walls and tries to talk with them about their actual lives: an upcoming war, the death of friends, family, politics. The women are indifferent to anything beyond the pleasures of the moment, and horrified when Montag fetches a hidden book of poetry and reads the poem "Dover Beach" ("where ignorant armies clash by night"). Mildred is so shaken that she locks herself in the bathroom and downs sleeping pills.

This scene haunted me, as you might expect, because I often felt a mild version of this dynamic playing out when I tried to talk with friends and relatives and even strangers about the 2016 election. It was impossible to have a serious discussion because they refused to take the election seriously.

This divide struck me as more profound than any other. It's certainly possible to view the election as a contest between the interests and sensibilities of electoral factions, with the result hinging on inflamed bigotries or insurgent rage. But what if Trumpism represented something more fundamental: the triumph of unseriousness?

I recognize that this word sounds imprecise, as well as condescending. Let me clarify. There were millions of voters who took the election incredibly *seriously*, who viewed it as a referendum on the American dream. But the number of voters who conducted a thorough and objective appraisal of how the candidate's policies would affect their lives was much smaller. Their seriousness was *attitudinal*, constructed largely in relation to their inner lives.

When I use the term *serious*, I'm not talking about attitude but a particular style of cognition whose constituent parts include critical thought, intellectual rigor, and (oh what the hell) the engagement of one's moral imagination.

The most glaring example of this cultural deficiency came in the form of the 42 percent of eligible voters who neglected to exercise their franchise at all, a figure that dwarfed the tally of the winning candidate. What should we call these citizens? *Unserious* strikes me as a generous assessment.

But I'm more interested in how this word describes the climate in which American democracy now struggles to persevere, and in particular how an ethically unfettered brand of capitalism has led us to transform ourselves from citizens into consumers ready to embrace our elections as entertainment products.

◆ ◆ ◆

In mulling all this, I dug out a battered copy of Neil Postman's *Amusing Ourselves to Death: Public Discourse in the Age of Show Business*. I remembered the book, published in 1985, as an elegant polemic against television. But Postman's concern is more profound. Like Bradbury, he sees the gradual abdication of moral and intellectual rigor as the greatest risk to American democracy. Postman outlines the deterioration of our national standards with such eerie precision that Trumpism comes to seem not only plausible but inevitable.

The book began as a lecture delivered at the Frankfort Book Fair. Postman was supposed to discuss Orwell's *1984*.

But he argued that the America of 1984 could be better understood by examining Aldous Huxley's *Brave New World*:

"In Huxley's vision, no Big Brother is required to deprive people of their autonomy, maturity and history. As he saw it, people will come to love their oppression, to adore the technologies that undo their capacities to think," Postman observes. "Orwell feared those who would deprive us of information. Huxley feared those who would give us so much that we would be reduced to passivity and egoism. Orwell feared that the truth would be concealed from us. Huxley feared the truth would be drowned in a sea of irrelevance. Orwell feared we would become a captive culture. Huxley feared we would become a trivial culture. . . . In short, Orwell feared that what we fear will ruin us. Huxley feared that what we desire will ruin us."

I believe Postman is largely right here. But his formulation overlooks the dark possibility that fear and desire might act in concert to undermine our democratic achievements. Americans find extraordinary pleasure in fear and loathing. Is there any other logical explanation for the stylish nightmares that dominate our popular culture, the networks that retail panic day and night?

◆ ◆ ◆

Postman believes our mass media has created a society whose standard of value is "whether or not something can grab and then hold the public's attention. It is a society in which those things that do not conform—for example, serious literature, serious political debate, serious ideas, serious anything—are more likely to be compromised or marginalized than ever before."

The result is that every aspect of our culture (politics, religion, news, education, commerce) has been "transformed into congenial adjuncts of show business, largely without protest or even much popular notice . . . When cultural life is redefined as a perpetual round of entertainments, when serious public conversation becomes a form of baby-talk, when, in short, a people become an audience, and their public business a vaudeville act, then a nation finds itself at risk; culture-death is a clear possibility."

Postman was hardly the first to offer this critique. "The people who run the mass media and those who consume it are really in the same boat," James Baldwin observed in 1959. "They must continue to produce things they do not really admire, still less love, in order to continue buying things they do not really want, still less need. If we were dealing only with fintails, two-tone cars, or programs like *Gunsmoke*, the situation would not be so grave. The trouble is that serious things are handled (and received) with the same essential lack of seriousness."

Postman conceived of his book to reckon with the reality that *Gunsmoke* had infiltrated the Oval Office. For the first time in American history, the president was not a lawyer or a general but a retired movie actor. To his credit, Ronald Reagan served two terms as governor of a large state. But Postman's thesis was that public figures were no longer judged on experience and competence. "In America, God favors all those who possess both a talent and a format to amuse."

Trumpism offers the most blatant example of this maxim to date. The candidate's training as a tabloid and TV star endowed him with the talent. Our Fourth Estate—cable news in particular—supplied him the format. From the moment he entered the race, the networks aired his speeches, fulminated over his antics, and promoted his tweets in shrieking chyron, as if they were major policy statements. In other words, they treated him like a celebrity.

If they had accorded him the coverage of a traditional politician—like, say, Jeb Bush—Trump never would have claimed the GOP nomination. His inexperience and erratic nature would have reduced him to a fringe candidate. He became the front-runner in large part because he was treated as the front-runner.

Nor did the networks make any secret of this double standard. Here's how CBS Chairman Les Moonves described Trump's run in February of 2016, speaking at a media conference sponsored by Morgan Stanley: "It may not be good for America, but it's damn good for CBS." Moonves went on to characterize the campaign as a "circus" but insisted "Donald's place in this election is a good thing. Man, who would have expected the ride we're all having right now? . . . The money's rolling in and this is fun. I've never seen anything like this, and this is going to be a very good year for us. Sorry. It's a terrible thing to say. But, bring it on, Donald. Keep going."

Moonves is telling himself at least two bad stories here. The first is that the short-term profit of his company is worth whatever long-term damage might be wrought by promoting a candidate so ill-equipped to assume the presidency. The second bad story, which helps him take such a jocular tone in announcing his moral bankruptcy, is that Trump can't possibly win. This was the story adopted by virtually every member of the media (myself included) to justify the disproportionate attention we devoted to his candidacy.

But there's a third bad story embedded in the Moonves statement: that the 2016 campaign was a "circus" that somehow took shape apart from the media, which merely observed the crazy doings under the big tent. In its own way, this was the most insidious story of all, because it allowed intelligent, principled reporters and producers and news executives to disavow their true role: they produced the circus and collected at the gate.

Trump's personal power over the media—his ability to do or say anything he wanted and still get coverage—was especially potent to voters who felt a keen sense of their own cultural impotence. Trump's prestige allowed them to feel they were part of a movement, despite the ideologically incoherent nature of his positions.

◆ ◆ ◆

Postman spends much of *Amusing* tracing the origin and meaning of our "descent into triviality." It begins, in his estimation, with the telegraph, a device that initiated our "vast and trembling shift from the magic of writing to the magic of electronics." By moving decontextualized information over great distances at incredible speed, the telegraph depicted a world as something to be consumed rather than experienced. Knowledge became drained of meaning, and disconnected from meaningful action. This led to what Postman calls "a great loop of impotence: The news elicits from you a variety of opinions about which you can do nothing except to offer them as more news, about which you can do nothing."

If the telegraph fractured our capacity to understand and engage with world events, television eviscerated it. Postman presents the medium much as Bradbury did: an alternate reality artfully designed to subdue a population on behalf of

the sponsors. He is especially brutal when it comes to assess-
ing television news:

> What is happening here is that television is altering the mean-
> ing of "being informed" by creating a species of information
> that might properly be called disinformation. I am using this
> word almost in the precise sense in which it is used by spies in
> the CIA or KGB. Disinformation does not mean false informa-
> tion. It means misleading information—misplaced, irrelevant,
> fragmented or superficial information—information that cre-
> ates the illusion of knowing something but which in fact leads
> one away from knowing.

None of this was deliberate, Postman observed. It was the
inexorable result of news packaged as entertainment. "In
saying that the television news show entertains but does not
inform, I am saying something far more serious than that
we are being deprived of authentic information. I am saying
we are losing our sense of what it means to be well informed.
Ignorance is always correctable. But what shall we do if we
take ignorance to be knowledge?"

Trumpism was like a stress test grimly designed to confirm Postman's theses. Day after day, the candidate and the
campaign floated conspiracy theories and inflammatory
smears. Rather than labeling them as false and moving on
to more substantive matters, such as policy, the networks

assembled panels to debate these claims for days, slickly re-packaging campaigns of misinformation as "controversies."

CNN President Jeff Zucker recently described his pro-Trump panelists to a reporter as "characters in a drama ... Everybody says, 'Oh, I can't believe you Jeffery Lord or Kayleigh McEnany,' but you know what? They know who Jeffrey Lord and Kayleigh McEnany are." When Postman complained, three decades ago, that television reduced journalism to show business, could he have foreseen the chief executive at a major network offering such a blithe confirmation?

◆ ◆ ◆

Postman's ultimate concern was epistemological. Television news, in seeking to entertain, no longer helped its audience make distinctions between justified belief and opinion. But the same complaint can be lodged against other media. I've smashed my dashboard a thousand times over the past decade upon hearing some politely droning NPR report that consists of:

- ► The introduction of a policy debate
- ► A conservative mouthing a talking point
- ► A liberal mouthing a talking point
- ► An anodyne observation about partisan divisions
- ► A summation of "it remains to be seen" or "only time will tell."

There is a name for this pablum. It's called *passive news reporting*. It's what happens when journalistic outlets don't have the resources, or the inclination, or the financial incentive, to investigate and resolve underlying factual disputes in a story. Many of our most revered newspapers practice passive news reporting because editors continue to define objectivity as the effort to present "both sides" of the story without regard to veracity. The proliferation of political fact checking columns is a symptom of this feckless reporting.

Hunter S. Thompson took this a step further. He called objective journalism "a pompous contradiction in terms." But passive reporting isn't even objectivity. It's dereliction of duty. And it damages our discourse. Citizens who consume passive reporting come to "feel like they can't figure out what the truth is," according to Raymond Pingree, a professor of communication at Ohio State University, who conducted a study of passive news reporting. "This attitude may lead people to tune out politics entirely, or to be more accepting of dishonesty by politicians."

◆ ◆ ◆

When politicians and their surrogates lie, and when media companies reward them with coverage for those lies, they are not simply providing a distraction from dubious policies and corruption. The coverage distorts people's beliefs, because repeating false claims over and over—even when you are debunking them—reinforces their validity.

The so-called illusory truth effect, first documented in the 1970s, is based on a cognitive quirk: when we hear a claim for the second or third (or tenth) time, our brains are quicker to respond to it, and we mistake this as a signal for it being true. The Yale psychologist Gordon Pennycook ran an experiment to test this premise, using fake news headlines from the 2016 campaign. The results replicated previous studies: subjects who read a false headline ("Pope Endorses Trump") were more likely to accept it as true later on, even when researchers slapped a warning on the bogus headlines—"Disputed by 3rd Party Fact-Checkers," the same caveat used by Facebook.

As a marketing savant, Trump surely understood the power of repeating debunked stories and crass labels ("Crooked Hillary"). He may even have read the seminal 2005 research paper *How Warnings about False Claims Become Recommendations*: "Telling people that a consumer claim is false can make them misremember it as true . . . Repeatedly identifying a claim as false helped older adults remember it as false in the short term but paradoxically made them more likely to remember it as true after a three-day delay. This unintended effect of repetition comes from increased familiarity with the claim itself but decreased recollection of the claim's original context."

A recent study by researchers at UCLA revealed that conservatives are more apt to believe false claims that suggest dangerous or apocalyptic outcomes. As one social scientist put it, delicately, "a lot of citizens are especially vigilant about potential threats but not especially motivated or prepared to process information in a critical, systematic manner."

This is what I meant when I said earlier that Americans savor their fears. (Why debunk that which secretly pleases you?) One can see this most flagrantly in conservative media outlets that specialize in paranoid insinuation, but also in mainstream media that repackage these bad stories.

A month after the election, the *Economist* commissioned a study of 1,376 Americans to gauge belief in various conspiracies. Trump voters believed:

► Obama was born in Kenya (48 percent)
► Leaked emails from Clinton staffers contained code words for pedophilia, human trafficking, and Satanic ritual abuse (53 percent)
► Millions of illegal votes were cast in the election (38 percent)
► Vaccines cause autism (69 percent)

But about a fifth of Clinton voters also believed the stuff about Satanic ritual abuse, and vaccines, and illegal votes.

This is precisely what Postman means when he talks about how television news *leads one away from knowing*.

It is also what Orwell meant when he wrote this: "The very concept of objective truth is fading out of the world. Lies will pass into history."

◆ ◆ ◆

Postman's ideas helped me see in a new light the episode that spurred Trump to run for president. Back in April of 2011, then Citizen Trump attended the White House Correspondents' Dinner as a guest of the *Washington Post*. For weeks, he had been raising his profile in conservative circles by reviving the birther conspiracy that Obama was born in Kenya. The president responded, that night, with a riff that mocked Trump not for being a bigot or a liar or even a bully, but for being . . . an unserious person:

> But all kidding aside, we all know about your credentials and breadth of experience. [Laughter.] For example—no, seriously, just recently, in an episode of *Celebrity Apprentice*—[laughter]—at the steakhouse, the men's cooking team did not impress the judges from Omaha Steaks. And there was a lot of blame to go around. But you, Mr. Trump, recognized that the real problem was a lack of leadership. And so ultimately, you didn't blame Lil' Jon or Meatloaf. [Laughter.] You fired Gary Busey. [Laughter.] And these are the kind of decisions that

would keep me up at night. [Laughter and applause.] Well handled, sir. [Laughter.] Well handled.

Trump had arrived expecting to be anointed an insider, only to discover that he was the evening's punch line, made sport of by the debonair African American president he had slandered, laughed at by the political and media elite.

The entire 2016 election can be seen as a revenge fantasy to this humiliation. On the night in question, Trump slinked off to lick his wounds. But five years later, he would channel his volcanic rage at Obama and his cadre by turning their mature democracy into *his* punch line. He did so by demonstrating that the true seat of American power no longer resides in the parlors of Washington, DC, but within the confines of our own parlor screens. In that realm, Trump's starring turn in *The Apprentice* was no joke. It was as vital to his success as his incendiary rhetoric.

For one thing, the franchise refurbished Trump's public image. In 2004, when the show debuted, Trump was a real estate developer on the downside of his career, one whose serial bankruptcies had reduced him to a brand manager. In the public imagination, he was a garish creature of the New York tabloids. *The Apprentice* managed both to humanize and aggrandize him. Enthroned in his oak-paneled boardroom, Trump played the ultimate corporate monarch, with the power to bless or banish. Contestants didn't compete for cash. They vied for a job in the Trump Organization. To be in his world defined success.

Trump himself came off as a tough but compassionate boss. He asked questions, sought the counsel of his advisers, and deftly arbitrated disputes between his subjects. He fired the weak and unworthy but did so with regret more often than malice.

Obama dismissed the show as a frivolous capitalist fantasia. But 28 million Americans tuned into the finale of the premier season. What they saw was a no-nonsense evangelist for the gospel of success. NBC beamed Trump into American homes every week for fourteen seasons.

Those who have never been able to fathom how quickly Trump's populist appeal took root, and how stubborn it has proved, would do well to recognize the mythic power television wields in our culture, the power to forge intimate hero figures who are absorbed into our psychic lives in ways we only half understand. To his fans, Trump was a far more persuasive figure than the unctuous strivers who invaded cable every four years to plead for votes. He was the consummate CEO come to fix the failing business known as America.

In a twist Postman might have foreseen, the man who signed Trump to his *Apprentice* gig was a programming guru named Jeff Zucker who would later take the helm at CNN and refashion the network into a much grander Trump reality show.

BAD STORY #7

JOURNALISM WOULD MAKE
A HERO OF ME

If I appear especially harsh toward our Fourth Estate in these pages, it's partly because I spent the first half of my adult life almost comically devoted to the belief that journalism would preserve American democracy. I still believe in the sacred duties of a free press. But if I'm honest about my own experiences in the field, the lessons that emerge most vividly are these:

1. Reporters are no more virtuous than anyone else, and often less so
2. Journalism hardly ever tells the most important stories
3. Even when it does, not much happens

◆ ◆ ◆

Consider this story: the summer before my last year in college, I took an internship at the Meriden *Record-Journal*, a tiny paper in central Connecticut. I was asked, toward the end of my tenure, to undertake what sounded like an ambitious project: documenting 24 hours in the life of the city. I was teamed with a veteran reporter named Richard Hanley, an energetic psychopath who sustained himself on a diet of steamed cheeseburgers and Kent cigarettes and who, wisely, consigned me to the graveyard shift.

Had I been serious about this assignment, I would have consulted with police, city officials, maybe a historian to map out an itinerary. I would have hung out with workers on an overnight factory shift, tagged along with a cop, visited an emergency room or a jail or a radio station or a homeless shelter. Instead, I spent most of the night camped in diners and donut shops, cadging quotes from bleary waitresses, then roaming the empty downtown waiting, I suppose, for the essence of Meriden, Connecticut, to descend from the dark summer sky and reveal itself, like an archangel. I eventually retired to the bucket seats of my Mercury Bobcat.

This piece stays with me, I think, because it begins to capture the audacious fallacy at the heart of modern journalism, the idea that a subjective (and frankly haphazard) account of one night in Meriden, compiled by a lazy 20-year-old who has never even lived in the city, can be touted as a definitive version of the place.

Or maybe the lesson is this: my bosses actually liked the story I handed in. The executive editor later called me into his office. He was a towering, silver-haired reptile, reviled by that entire small, ill-tempered newsroom. But he looked upon me fondly, probably because I was obsequious and poorly dressed. He floated the idea that I drop out of school and come to work full-time for him. When I demurred—and this part of the story I've never quite figured out—he slipped me an envelope with $350 cash inside. "Go buy something for your girlfriend," he murmured mystically. "Go get her some cocaine."

◆ ◆ ◆

After college, I took a job as a features reporter and rock critic at the *El Paso Times*. Like most Americans, I had never lived on the U.S./Mexico border. My balcony afforded me a view of the Rio Grande, across which Mexican day maids waded each dawn with plastic bags on their heads. They would scramble up the concrete embankment to the American side and pull dry work clothes out of these plastic bags and change into them. Sometimes it was cold and they shivered. Sometimes, a pale green INS van would show up and chase them through the low desert scrub. I watched all this from my balcony, as I sipped coffee. Then I drove into the office to interview the newest member of the boy band New Kids on the Block.

That was what my bosses wanted. I didn't recognize it at the time—I was too busy swanning around town, flashing my business card and abusing adjectives—but journalism was undergoing a paradigm shift. Corporations were swooping in to snap up dailies and consolidate them into chains. Catch phrases such as *news you can use* had begun to infiltrate the newsroom. Barely a decade removed from Watergate, papers were losing audience share to television, and they responded by adopting the look and the values of television. The flagship of our chain, *USA Today*, was a splashy "media product" dominated by color graphics, photos, sports, and celebrities, with a dash of news.

The staffers at the *El Paso Times* weren't callous or dumb. They simply worked for a company whose aim was to generate revenues from a dwindling readership, and which therefore devoted only a fraction of its resources to telling the essential story of the border—the perverse morality that abounds when privilege and poverty collide.

My girlfriend at the time worked as an independent radio reporter. One night she drove down to the International Bridge to cover a wildcat strike by Mexican chili pickers and called me a few hours later, in distress, to report that the police had beaten up some of the strikers, and their family members. By the time I arrived the fracas was all over. Only a few broken signs remained, along with a dozen chili pickers who still wanted to get in a day of labor. They had slipped over from Juarez in the dark and were sleeping on the sidewalks of South El Paso, curled like question marks on flats of cardboard, young men mostly, around my age. At four a.m., a line of school buses showed up and drove them two hours north to the fields of southern New Mexico, where they filled buckets for ten hours, until their sinuses burned with chili oil. The pickers were paid 40 cents per bucket. As I recall, the strikers were agitating for 43 cents per bucket.

I wrote all this up later, in an urgent little memo, and whisked it over to the City Editor, assuming it would wind up on the front page. A small item about the "disturbance" appeared inside the metro section.

◆ ◆ ◆

I don't mean to suggest that no one was writing stories of substance. My friend Paul Salopek produced dozens of investigative stories, about abuses by the border patrol, the inhalant epidemic, the lives of transvestite prostitutes in Juarez. (He would go on to win two Pulitzer Prizes at the *Chicago Tribune*.) Paul churned through mountains of data. He called hundreds of sources. He spent weeks with his subjects. He filed Freedom of Information Act requests. He filled hundreds of notebooks. Then he pulled all-nighters to distill this material into pieces that might fit within a dwindling news hole. Paul was an outlier, a journalist who produced serious work within an inherently unserious system.

Inspired and perhaps shamed by him, I occasionally tried to take my job more seriously. The story that comes to mind was an exposé about print journalism in Juarez, which I portrayed as hopelessly corrupt. Reporters, I suggested, were little more than PR agents hired out to the highest bidder. One major paper was funded by drug money. I made it all sound pretty explosive.

The staggering irony here is that the story was riddled with errors. My Spanish was rudimentary at best. I fumbled through interviews, using a Mexican reporter for a leftist paper as my emergency translator, and massaging quotes. I reported rumors as fact. The *Times* published all of it.

Within hours, I had been summoned by the publisher and asked to produce my notebooks. At some point, a quartet of indignant Mexican reporters appeared in our newsroom. They were led to the conference room for a meeting to which I was not invited. Lawyers were involved now. The *Times* eventually published a long public apologia, penned by the publisher himself.

I should have been summarily fired. But the matter blew over and I returned, chastened but unscathed, to the province of glitz.

◆ ◆ ◆

I left El Paso to take a job at an alternative weekly in Miami called the *New Times*. For four years, I spent most of my professional life documenting the misdeeds of crooked cops and con artists, shady developers and city officials. South

Florida was a swamp of depravity and the overriding mission at the paper was to expose the systemic flaws that allowed it to flourish.

Reporters at the *Miami Herald* often derided the *New Times* because the paper was free. But alt weeklies provided young reporters like me the time and space to tell complex stories. If we needed a month to get all the documents, to track down the sources, to make sense of what it all meant, we could have a month. If it took 5,000 words to get it right, we could have that, too. There were moments when I thought I'd found my calling.

I can remember spending hours in the basement of a county clerk's office outside Fort Lauderdale squinting at reams of microfilm. I was hunting for court records related to the billionaire sports team owner Wayne Huizenga, about whom I was compiling an unauthorized biography. I eventually came upon a 1961 civil suit filed by a man who claimed that a young Huizenga had showed up on his doorstep, selling a trash-hauling service. When the plaintiff demurred, Huizenga attacked his potential customer, causing broken sunglasses, abrasions on his face, and, most memorably, "permanent injury to the testicles and genital area as a result of grabbing and twisting by the defendant." This turned out to be a rather neat summary of his modus operandi as a businessman.

Gradually, though, I began to lose my sense of mission. My editors wanted indictments. That's what made readers pick up the paper. But pursuing subjects in this way made me feel predatory. The hows and whys of corruption began to strike me as far less compelling than *why* people self-destructed in the first place.

It was the same feeling I'd gotten in El Paso: that the accounts in newspapers, valuable as they could be, rarely touched the truth of what it means to be a human. There were all these sad, private moments that never made it into print. I had begun reading and writing fiction by then to help make sense of such moments, and I turned my attention to stories that allowed me to express my literary ambitions.

I remember, in particular, the months I spent writing about the James E. Scott Homes, a public housing project in Liberty City that residents called the Canyon. Most news reports about the Canyon focused on car jackings that transpired on the surrounding avenues. But I was interested in the daily life of the place, a vast archipelago of housing units filled with dejected moms and their restive children.

Because there were almost no dads around, I fell into the habit of taking a group of boys on little weekend excursions— to the movies, to the library, to the beach. One Saturday, I drove them down to the zoo in South Dade. On the way back, my car ran out of gas right in the middle of I-95. I managed to coast onto a thin shoulder. Instantly, it began to rain with a cinematic intensity. Eighteen-wheelers hurtled past, blasting water against our windows.

This was before cell phones existed, so I told my terrified charges—they ranged in age from eight to ten—that I would go find gas and that they should stay put. I tumbled down an embankment, scaled a fence, and jogged around in a panic. Eventually, I paid two guys forty bucks for a gallon of gas and a ride back to my car, which, naturally, I could not locate. We spent half an hour circling that infernal knot of highways before I finally spotted my little Tercel.

The kids were ecstatic. Two of them had been crying. "See, I told you he was coming back!" said a third. The men who had rescued me were stunned, or probably closer to appalled. "Them boys could have been killed," one of them murmured.

It occurred to me, rather dimly, that if a police car had spotted my vehicle and pulled over to check it out, I might be facing a criminal charge of child endangerment, or even kidnapping. What was my standing here, after all? I wasn't a social worker or a Big Brother or even a family friend. I was a reporter who had taken these boys on a kind of joyride so that later I could write about their suffering.

I spent more than a year visiting those boys and when, at last, the joyride was over, my story came out. It recorded many of the most harrowing scenes I'd witnessed in the Canyon, unguarded moments in which a mother or auntie struck her child, or the rotting body of a grandmother was discovered, or an infant left to wail. I was trying to be honest about what happens when poverty and despair collide. But the piece did nothing to change the lives of those boys, or their guardians. It merely held them up for public inspection and won me a few accolades.

It might be said that I'd finally learned to take journalism seriously and that journalism had returned the favor by revealing its most serious lesson: that it could, on occasion, hold the powerful to account. But that it could not awaken the conscience of the powerful, nor rescue those most in need.

The Canyon was an important story to tell, maybe the most important one I've ever told. It was also the last piece I ever wrote as a full-time reporter.

NOBODY WOULD VOTE
FOR A GUY LIKE THAT

In turning away from daily journalism, I did not abandon my investigation of the American story. Nor could I have. Writers wind up chasing their white whales, like it or not. All I did was shift the means of my pursuit to fiction and essays.

Given my lifelong obsession with the power and frailty of the Fourth Estate, it will come as no surprise that my first novel, a disastrous 190,000-word bildungsroman, arose from my journalistic misadventures in El Paso. My hero, a glib young reporter at a border newspaper, fabricates a florid feature story that runs on the front page. Naturally, he gets found out and banished to the copy desk. He eventually goes berserk, quite boringly: skips out on his job, betrays his girlfriend, meets an old Mexican shaman who heals him—just the sort of twists you'd expect from a rookie novelist with the gifts of a middling memoirist.

As a character, my protagonist is painfully unconvincing, and infatuated by his own glib banter. But as a spokesman for my anxieties about the decline of print journalism, he has his moments. He can see that newspapers are imperiled, not by the recklessness of show-offs like him, but the frantic pace of digital culture and the merciless incentives of the free market.

As my anguish about our civic life escalated, I began to churn out a steady stream of essays and editorials lamenting the cynicism overtaking us as a people, the expansion of the right-wing media, and its outsized influence over our discourse. I was particularly agitated by the rise of the Tea Party.

Like a lot of naïve liberals, I'd initially viewed the movement as the plaything of corporate interests, a pale mob riled up by billionaire PACs and Fox News hoopla. Their signs, festooned with swastikas and hammers and sickles, bearing slogans such as KEEP GOVT OUT OF MY MEDICARE and OBAMA'S PLAN: WHITE SLAVERY, made it tough to take them seriously as political actors. But the 2010 midterms had proven that it was possible to dominate media coverage, and to win elections, without being informed or even especially coherent.

The Tea Party represented a strain of American fundamentalism, one that converted feelings of declining utility into heroic victimhood. Its aims were political but its means were emotional. And I could see that a determined operator would be able to capitalize on all this, especially if he knew how to manipulate the media.

And so I began to write a novel about a hedonistic, right-wing demagogue named Bucky Dunn who decides to run for president and shocks everyone, himself included, by nearly winning the GOP nomination. I hoped to have a draft ready in time for the 2016 election. But I fell out of love with my hero—always a fatal blow to works of imagination.

For reasons I hope are understandable, I couldn't bring myself to look at the manuscript during the campaign. Nor did I need to. Bucky Dunn's code of conduct—manic self-promotion, gluttony, screen addiction, sexual predation, casual racism—was on display everywhere I looked. Bucky sounded nothing like a right-wing demagogue. But his shtick on the stump sounded all the same themes: *The nation is in flames. The media is corrupt. The elites are mocking you.* Eerily, I'd even written a Trump cameo into the book, after Bucky visits one of his resorts:

> Trump had refurbished a mile of coastline, rendering what had been a haven for seagulls and their filthy ways into a world-class destination . . . This was a golf course, an Eden beyond the jurisdiction of public sector employees. The grass exhaled oxygen and the oligarchs made gentle thwacks. Some-where close by, quail were being spun in centrifuges and re-leased to the heavens. At each tee, a video of Trump greeted

us, his lovely anus of a mouth extruding promotional syllables, his delicate hair panels radiating deserved self-love.

◆ ◆ ◆

Anyone who's been tracking the convergence of America's conservative media and its broader political theater could have confected Bucky Dunn. He's simply coming at the scam from the opposite direction of folks such as Mike Huckabee and Sarah Palin.

He spends the early sections of the book barnstorming cable TV shows from the back of his massive SUV, which he's converted into a portable studio. He knows that folks who feel looked down upon crave the malignant charms of the bully so he stages feuds on Twitter and hijacks news cycles by making outrageous accusations (the president has erectile dysfunction). Rather than delivering formal speeches, he holds raucous rallies in swing state arenas. He dreams of re-purposing the presidency as a platform for a raft of reality TV programs.

Bucky has a long history of womanizing, drinking, and making offensive statements. But he promotes these coarse behaviors as proof of his authenticity. ("My sins were my assets. The worse I behaved, the better my hotel room. It was an absurd and thrilling arrangement.") Bucky intuits what Trump would affirm: that contempt for the political and media classes is so intense among certain voters as to cancel out issues of character or competence. He dominates the debates by making brash statements, to the ecstasy of his intended audience: GOP primary voters.

In a culture impervious to serious discourse, why shouldn't a guy like Bucky take his shot? What's the point of writing the script for your followers, if you can't play the leading role?

Bucky is ultimately undone by his addiction to attention, which lures him into appearing on a program called *The Gauntlet*, where all his most damning secrets are revealed: that he lied about his history, that he once experimented with homosexuality, that he pressured his ex-wife to get an abortion. Bucky comes to realize that he's been played by conspirators who promoted then torpedoed his campaign. He flies into a rage, assaults the host on live TV, and winds up in prison.

It's a liberal wish fantasy.

◆ ◆ ◆

So what became of the novel? This part of the story is a bit more complicated. Essentially, my readers felt Bucky was too cruel and cartoonish. Nobody would vote for a guy like that. And nobody, I was assured, would root for a character like that. And so I began to second guess my hero. Or rather, I began to encumber him. I handed him a young son to parent and an estranged daughter who was kidnapped by Somali pirates in early drafts, and later morphed into a recovering addict. Bucky became more "sympathetic," but in the process—and there's a cruel lesson here, for those not afraid to see it—he became less compelling.

This is what I meant when I said I fell out of love with Bucky. I'd conceived of him, consciously, as the embodiment of our civic dysfunction. But I also adored his misbehavior, his appetites, his joyous repudiation of liberal guilt. I'd created Bucky to enact my own repressed urges. Then I'd strangled the life out of him, using my superego as the murder weapon.

Bucky was trying to tell me something: that we had moved beyond truth and shame in American politics. But I refused to listen. He was the part of me, of all of us maybe, who awaited the arrival of Donald Trump. I don't mean the folks who fed off his hate or fell for his pitch or even the ones who subjugated their common sense to tribal allegiance. I mean the other 73 percent of us, who couldn't look away from the spectacle, who kept pumping the oxygen of attention into his crusade. We told ourselves a bad story: that he would inevitably crash, and that his crash would serve as a tough but necessary lesson in the resilience of American democracy. We refused to accept that Trump might be starring in a story of his own, an epic about the power of unbridled aggression.

We forgot about Ahab, up on deck, roaring at his crew. "Talk not to me of blasphemy, man; I'd strike the sun if it insulted me."

I DO GET A LOT OF HONESTY
ON THE INTERNET

In the months before I quit my job in Miami to pursue literary obscurity, a number of people in the newsroom began talking about something called "The Web" or sometimes, more mysteriously, "The Internet." Kyle, the Texan ad rep, swore it was going to change the very nature of our lives. People would be able to put photos and maps and articles on the web and anyone else with a computer could see these things. I didn't get it. Why would people look at these things on a computer? They already existed. Kyle's face got redder and redder. "You don't understand," he said. "You're not seeing it."

I'm pretty sure Kyle now owns an island.

Our editor-in-chief certainly saw it. He would often drag reporters into his bayfront office so as to inflict upon them an ardent tutorial on the joy of hyperlinks—ironic, given that the Internet would decimate the economic base of his newspaper within a few years.

But I want to be careful to avoid portraying the Internet as the grand culprit in our cultural decay. That's a bad story, as hokey as the notion that the Internet would make us a more informed and unified population. The Internet is a tool. It can't make us dumb or shallow or mean. It can only enable these outcomes.

What the Internet has done is accelerate the pace of informational self-determination. Rather than letting Walter Cronkite tell us "And that's the way it is," the web lets us "have it our way." We gobble up new items that satisfy our emotional hungers without being factually or intellectually nutritious.

Americans have long hankered for such junk. Even in the age of Lincoln and Douglas, when broadsheets published direct transcriptions of their eloquent debates, there was also plenty of yellow journalism. Over the past half century, this tabloid style has come to be the dominant mode of the Fourth Estate. There is still serious reporting devoted to the common crises of state, and potential policy remedies. But as Postman noted, these reports now drift in a sea of frantic hype.

It has come to seem normal, for instance, that coverage of the first presidential debate would focus on how much one candidate sniffed into his microphone, and how much the other smiled, while not a single question was posed to either about the most urgent threat to our planet. In fact, not one of the three debates included a question about climate change.

What this shift represents, rather than any concerted plan, is simply the levers of capitalism treating "news" and "information" as a market rather than as a civic institution. Editors must now ask: *Does this story stimulate?* Will it convert attention into ad revenue? When the value of a story is measured in clicks, editorial judgment becomes an algorithm. There is no higher standard. We have been left to our own devices. The Internet is our ultimate device.

◆ ◆ ◆

If, as Postman argues, television delivers us facts with little sense of their moral significance or historical context, our reliance on the Internet has created a more troubling paradigm, an inverted epistemology in which we seek out propaganda and propaganda, in turn, seeks us out.

To take an obvious example, consider all those who were unsettled by Obama's election. Where had this bi-racial Hussein come from? Obama's life was thoroughly documented. But those driven by racial and religious anxiety could turn to the Internet to find "sources" that cast doubt on his biography, sources eventually amplified by the networks and newspapers. When Obama entered office, just 10 percent of Republicans believed he was Muslim. During his last year in office, more than half did, including two-thirds of Trump voters.

The goal of the large corporations who preside over most of the Internet is not to deliver us the truth, but to keep us on their platforms as long as possible. To do this, algorithms study our patterns, then fill our social media feeds and search result pages with items that will confirm, rather than challenge, our biases—even when this means promoting fake news.

Of course, there are two ways to be fooled, as Kierkegaard observed: "One is to believe what isn't true; the other is to refuse to believe what is true." The Internet facilitates both.

This is a big reason why the American public is so misinformed on basic issues of fact. Two-thirds of Trump voters believe unemployment went up under Obama. (It was cut in half.) Four-in-ten believe the stock market went down. (It tripled from its low point during the recession). Nearly 80 percent believe crime became more pervasive during the Obama years. (It fell sharply.) We could go ticking down the list, from climate change to the popular vote tally to illegal immigration rates to voter fraud. This isn't a matter of conservatives cherry-picking stats, nor of facts being obscured or distorted by the entertainment impulse. This is a direct retailing of falsehoods and conspiracies as fact.

◆ ◆ ◆

If the Internet can be said to have an original intent, it was to facilitate the flow of information and discourse. Everyone would hang out in the same big bubble. There would be lots of cross-pollination. In practice, the Internet has delivered reams of unfiltered data and opinion into our palms, and individuals have responded by constructing tribal fortresses.

You can see this most plainly on social media, where partisans sort themselves into opposing echo chambers. These platforms are not journalistic organs. They're giant digital chat rooms where people post stuff. That's fine when stuff is a video of your kitten stalking a laser pen. But a growing number of Americans treat Facebook and Twitter as news sources. They spend hours reading, reacting to, and reposting articles that purport to be factual. These items are subject to almost no oversight. Many are deployed to serve a political end.

A team of Buzzfeed reporters studied which election stories garnered the most attention on Facebook. Early in the campaign, stories from venues such as the *New York Times* and the *Washington Post* dominated. But in the last three months of the campaign, the top twenty items produced by propagandists received more attention than the top twenty stories produced by journalists. Seventeen of these were pro-Trump, or anti-Clinton, all easily debunked.

To be clear: these stories were not simply unleashed onto the public. They were injected into the cultural bloodstream by obscure hyper-partisan or hoax sites, some, we now know,

launched by Russian operatives. Individual Americans—
most of them Trump voters—then blasted them hither and
yon. They used the Internet to organize themselves into a
DIY propaganda machine.

They did this, I suspect, as a way of responding to the
drumbeat of mainstream reports detailing Trump's corruption: the fraud charges, the bogus charity, the boasts
of sexual assault, etc. Rather than disputing the merits of
these stories, they created an alternative media ecosystem
in which Clinton's phony crimes were so outlandish as to
absolve Trump's indisputable misdeeds.

Why does Facebook allow this? Because Facebook is in
the business of aggregating attention, even if that means fos-
tering ideological conformity and hyper-partisan thought.

During the election and for months afterward, the heads
of our most popular social media platforms played dumb
when it came to their role as promoters of propaganda. Only
under explicit questioning by congressional panels did they
admit anything. Yes, Facebook received millions of dollars
to run thousands of racist, polarizing ads. Yes, those ads
came from Putin-approved sources. Yes, Russian trolls were
allowed to set up fake accounts. Yes, 120 million Americans
saw their disinformation. Yes, 30,000 Russian bots haunted
the digital halls of Twitter, trolling credulous Americans to
the tune of nearly 300 million views. Yes, Google bought the
same traitorous ads. And no, none of these companies sought

to safeguard their platforms from Russian infiltration, oversight being the enemy of market share and revenue.

◆ ◆ ◆

It's worth recalling here how much trouble Sarah Palin got
in during her notorious 2008 interview with Katie Couric,
in part because she was unwilling to specify where she got
her news. Trump suffers no such discretion. "Forget the press,
read the Internet," he told crowds on the campaign trail. "I
do get a lot of honesty over the Internet."

What Trump got on the Internet was self-serving disinformation, which he would repeat until it no longer served
his interests to do so. Sometimes this stuff was merely
self-aggrandizing. But sometimes the lies were more malignant. Trump tweeted a graphic claiming that 81 percent of
white murder victims are slain by African Americans. When
it was pointed out to him that the FBI puts the actual percentage at fourteen, he huffed, "I retweeted somebody that was
supposedly an expert. . . . Am I gonna check every statistic?"

The source for this datum, the Crime Statistic Bureau,
does not exist. But it got a huge bump from Trump's en-
dorsement. After his tweet, Google searches for "black on
white crime" tripled. When Trump first proposed a ban
on Muslims entering the United States, citing a hate group
called the Center for Security Policy (CSP), searches for that

group increased nearly tenfold, and traffic to the site—a repository for anti-Muslim conspiracy theories—spiked.

The net effect is that more people seek out bad stories. Misinformation becomes mainstreamed, consumed not by thousands but millions. The pursuit of knowledge becomes a process of self-indoctrination, one abetted by those profit-seeking algorithms.

◆ ◆ ◆

I saw this process play out firsthand with a young friend of mine named Jon. Like me, he began the 2016 election as an ardent supporter of Bernie Sanders. I saw him in June and was impressed by his political engagement. Here was a shy guy in his early twenties who spoke thoughtfully about economic injustice.

In the months after Clinton formally accepted the nomination, the nature of Jon's rhetoric changed. He began to respond to social media posts by friends and relatives with links to anti-Clinton pieces from strange websites. He often fired off these responses in the wee hours, with dire pronouncements about how the media wasn't covering the "real stories." I chalked up his behavior to disappointment, along with resentment (probably unconscious) toward his mother, an ardent Clinton supporter with whom he still lived.

We now know that Russian operatives, acting on orders from the Kremlin, bombarded guys like Jon with anti-Clinton agitprop throughout the campaign. This effort was part of what the *New York Times* called, back in 2015, "the biggest trolling operation in history," one aimed at decimating "the utility of the Internet as a democratic space."

When people hear allegations of cyber-terrorism, they envision high-tech operatives hacking into secured government servers. But the Russians recognized that American democracy was vulnerable to a far more humble approach. They "hacked" Bernie supporters by posting fake news stories on their Facebook pages, websites, and forums.

The Russians made a calculated bet that a guy like Jon, if sufficiently goaded, would shift from an agenda driven by progressive goals to one driven by animus toward Clinton. Jon professed disgust for Trump. But his Facebook page was filled with links to articles vilifying Clinton. The reports came from far-right websites, a Romanian fake news farm, a website affiliated with the Syrian dictator Bashar al-Assad. Taken together, Jon's posts composed a kind of ideologically incoherent gumbo in which the main ingredients were disinformation, distrust of authority in general, and Clinton in particular—the same stew Trump dished out daily at his rallies.

Jon didn't just opine on social media. He also participated in group chats, circulating these same links, while bantering with friends and relatives. Here, too, his logic was tough to follow. "This country can't survive another Clinton presidency," he wrote to his chat group, who all just happened to be female Clinton supporters. "Clinton will lead us into war. She'll create a corporatist controlled police state." When another member of his chat group asked him about the dangers of electing Trump, he replied, "Why are you stuck on fear mongering?"

I recognized Jon's rhetorical posture from my own years as a Ralph Nader crusader. He wanted to vote for someone he believed in, not the lesser of two evils. But his logic was that of a fatalist: the system was broken beyond repair, policies were empty promises to a wage slave like him.

The conservative movement fosters this false equivalence, which breeds apathy and depresses turnout. "A vote for hillary is a vote for trump," Jon wrote a few weeks before the election, which is how you know he isn't a person of color, or a Muslim, or an immigrant.

◆ ◆ ◆

A few days after the election, Jon asked his mother—who had spent election night in tears—whether it was weird that he felt elated by the results. When I heard about this comment, something clicked in my mind. Jon saw himself as an online activist committed to progressive causes. But more fundamentally, he was a high school grad stuck in his mom's house.

In this sense, he was part of a larger generational cohort: alienated young men who went online to find the power they couldn't experience in real life ("IRL").

They did this by congregating in digital communities, such as the message board 4chan.org, where they vied for attention by spouting invective. They banded together to form the hacker collective Anonymous and launched coordinated attacks on perceived enemies. The goal of these loose-knit networks was never political, because the "shitlords" who ruled these sites didn't believe in politics. But as the writer Dale Beran has observed, many embraced Trump "as a defiant expression of despair." They recognized him as an embodiment of their own adolescent nihilism. In exposing politics as a joke, he had trolled democracy.

I don't think Jon visited these sites. I only know that he spent hours upon hours online, absorbing agitprop aimed at him, and that he turned away from issues of economic uplift and committed himself, with increasing vigor, to trashing Clinton and agitating her voters.

This is why he felt elation at the election result: it had served as a final rebuke to his mother and all those other Hillary hags too dumb to recognize the folly of genuine political belief. Over the course of a single campaign, his immersion in internet culture had transformed him from an American idealist into a Russian bot.

◆ ◆ ◆

The Internet feeds this kind of aggrieved groupthink, particular among angry young men. It grants them the illusion of reportorial industry without any of the inconvenient moral or factual safeguards. In this way, it becomes the ideal breeding ground for radicalism, because users experience their indoctrination as a form of actualization. Here is how federal investigators described the mindset of Dylann Roof, the young man who slaughtered nine African-American parishioners in a church in Charleston, South Carolina in 2015:

"Every bit of motivation came from things he saw on the internet. That's it. . . . He is simply regurgitating, in whole paragraphs, slogans and facts—bits and pieces of facts that he downloaded from the Internet directly into his brain." Roof described being "truly awakened" by the shooting of Trayvon Martin, though what he meant was the precise moment he went online:

> This prompted me to type in the word "black on white crime" into Google, and I have never been the same since that day. The first website I came to was the Council of Conservative Citizens. There were pages upon pages of these brutal black on white murders. I was in disbelief. At this moment I realized that something was very wrong. How could the news be blow-

ing up the Trayvon Martin case while hundreds of these black on white murders got ignored?

Roof explained that he had no choice but to commit the murders. "We have no skinheads, no real KKK, no one doing anything but talking on the internet. Well someone has to have the bravery to take it to the real world, and I guess that has to be me."

The media faithfully treats the Dylann Roofs of the world as "lone gunmen." It's more comforting to see them as machines that malfunctioned rather than Americans who came to regard lethal violence as a means of political expression. But the Internet has provided angry and often isolated citizens a forum to flout this standard. Faced with a dearth of white supremacists in his area, Roof went online to seek validation. Duly validated, he took it to the real world.

Anyone who's visited a partisan chat room, or browsed the comments section at the bottom of an article, knows the Internet creates a safe space for sadism. We compete to shame and incite in anonymous forums. We insult people in ways we would never dare if we had to face them in person, and get cheered for doing so. The more time we spend on the Internet—the more we're exposed to, and participate in, unchecked contempt and uncontested lies—the more degraded our sense of common decency becomes.

One of the central revelations of the 2016 campaign was the extent to which Internet culture has forged an entirely new permission structure. Just try to imagine the reaction if Ronald Reagan mocked a disabled reporter or got caught bragging about grabbing pussy.

In a broader sense, our embrace of the Internet has deregulated the social contract. In our quest for open source knowledge we have created a public forum plagued by unsourced misinformation. In our yearning for connection, we have fashioned digital bunkers in which citizens sit alone for hours expressing primal negative emotions without fear of consequence, even with some hope of acclaim. This ethical bifurcation is the psychic fingerprint of the Internet. We have come to accept cruelty and deceit as inevitable in our civic life, and our leaders.

♦ ♦ ♦

This brings us to the alt-right, which functioned during the election as a kind of dark twin to establishment conservatism. Media outlets had a tough time defining the alt-right, because it's not really a political movement so much as a noisy counter culture whose ranks include racial extremists, reactionary academics, and basement-bound misogynists. The alt-right is what happens when fringe thinkers discover a cultural space where they can freely congregate, propagate ideas, and incite. Like the Islamists who use the Internet to recruit, alt-right culture appeals to young men hungry for the empowerment of radicalism.

A guy like my friend Jon would never endorse the anti-democratic ideas of the alt-right, at least at a family picnic. But when he goes online, he becomes part of a larger army that has failed to find a place within American liberal democracy and has decided, therefore, to burn it down.

They can't literally burn it down, of course. Unlike the radicals bred by ISIS, or the ones who took to the streets in the Sixties, the self-proclaimed shitlords of the alt-right can agitate from the safety of their bedrooms, by spattering social media and message boards with vile memes and slogans that openly traffic in fascism, eugenics, and violent misogyny.

Emergent media outlets such as Breitbart.com recognized the commercial potential in promoting this invective, and candidate Trump—safe in the knowledge that even moderate Republicans were too tribal to vote for Hillary—happily positioned himself as the ultimate shitlord. Mainstream media outlets were left to decode the symbology of the alt-right. The Clinton campaign, worried about meme warfare, released a document titled "Donald Trump, Pepe the frog, and white supremacists: an explainer." Thanks to the Internet, a bunch of alienated outsiders found themselves in the vanguard of American political discourse.

Many of them viewed politics as a joke. But the attention they garnered online was quickly exploited by ideologues with IRL political goals: a crackdown on immigration, economic and military isolationism, an aggressive dismantling of the federal government (i.e., "the administrative state").

Trump was hardly the first American politician to embrace these reactionary positions. But he was the first to do so with the help of the Internet, a realm where the naked cruelty and divisive cynicism of his oratory found a haven, and flourished.

◆ ◆ ◆

Because the Internet liberates the primal negative emotions that bubble beneath our public discourse, it is especially useful as a predictive tool.

I learned this firsthand a decade ago, when I began writing political commentary for the *Boston Globe* and other venues. My email inbox began to fill up with letters of a sort I had never encountered before. Letters may be dressing it up a bit. They were rants brimming with the sort of bile you never see on Fox News, whose glossy insinuations have been scrubbed for the sponsors.

Here's what I mean:

GET OUT OF AMERICA,

YOU ANTI-AMERICAN, NO GOOD, SCUM SUCKER!!!

I am sending your article in the Boston Globe to our troops in Iraq and Afghanistan. When I told them about it, via the internet, they all begged me to send them a copy. This I will gladly do. Lot of our men and women from Massachusetts are there now, and they are looking forward to meeting (finding) you! GET OUT OF AMERICA!!! YOU HAVE NO RIGHT LIVING HERE UNDER THE PROTECTION OF MEN AND WOMEN OF HONOR AND RESPECTABILITY WHILE YOU ARE NOTHING BUT A LOWLY, COWARDLY, INSECT!!

And:

Dear Asshole,

You are a fucking idiot!! And your daughter in the picture on your website looks like a maggot! You are a disgraceful american and it would have been so nice if you had been a passenger on one of the planes that crashed into one of the wtc towers on 9/11/01.

And:

If you liberals get your way and let others take down our country I wouldn't be sorry at all that you would end up in a work camp.

◆ ◆ ◆

Part of the reason I wasn't entirely shocked by Trump's rise is because I'd heard from his most ardent supporters already. I understood that lurking within the conservative movement was a faction of citizens who didn't care about free market evangelism or any other ideological pieties, who saw themselves, instead, as engaged in a struggle for national unity and purity. And who were ready to characterize any perceived enemy as vermin fit for transport to a work camp—at least on the Internet.

These letters could only have arisen from internet culture. They were impulsive reactions, hastily composed and fired off by individuals scowling into screens. The fact that my correspondents would never have delivered such messages in person didn't make them any less revelatory. It made them more so. It showed how little it took to liberate their authoritarian impulses.

David Neiwert's terrifying 2009 tract, *The Eliminationists: How Hate Talk Radicalized the American Right*, focuses on the pervasive use of violent rhetoric on the right and how it has bred a mindset that "always depicts its opposition as beyond the pale, the embodiment of evil itself—unfit for participation in their vision of society, and thus worthy of elimination. It often further depicts its designated Enemy as vermin."

The point of Neiwert's book is not that America is a fascist state but that voices on the far right (what was then the fringe) pushed an agenda in which violence against internal enemies was seen as not just acceptable, but vital.

◆ ◆ ◆

As a reminder, this is all happening in 2010. Donald Trump is still just a gaseous planet orbiting the tarnished sun of Reality TV.

Even back then, concealed in the dark matter of the Internet, his legions awaited him. They awaited his calls for savagery, his assassination fantasies. In a deeper sense, they awaited a politician who operated at the pace and pitch of the Internet, who put a kingly gloss on their own entrapped aggressions, their appetite for ad hominem, their contempt for weakling elites, their cleansing rage.

Trump not only rewarded them, but emerged as the first true Internet candidate. His campaign manager was an online provocateur. He lived deep within an informational silo, scoured the web for affirmations of his righteousness, and circumvented unfriendly media by tweeting directly to his people.

Neil Postman worried about facts getting drowned out in a "sea of irrelevance" on TV. What he could not have foreseen was a medium in which a presidential candidate could mount an assault on truth itself.

It's not just that the work of scientists and journalists now sits alongside the flimflam sponsored by partisan and corporate hacks in your Facebook feed. It's the realization that the Internet has allowed a growing number of Americans to abandon any standards of proof. In such a climate, what's to stop a presidential candidate from lying? From slandering opponents? From contradicting taped testimony? From fabricating job numbers or crime stats or terrorist attacks? So what if you get caught? You can just hop on the Internet and cast any denunciations as the handiwork of politically correct thought police who seek to silence you. By recasting censure as censorship, you can transmute vitriol into victimhood.

◆ ◆ ◆

Recognizing that the Internet is just a tool and that we all use it in different ways—to communicate, to educate ourselves, to peacefully masturbate—is it fair to define a troll as one who uses the Internet to convert private shame into public recrimination? Who locates power in the violation of decorum, and the infliction of humiliation? Should it shock any of us that Trump is conducting the business of the presidency in this frantic and furious style? What I'm suggesting is more profound: Trump conducts his life in this manner. He flits restlessly from one target to the next, energized by the agitation he causes, and egged on by sycophantic followers, whom he values chiefly for their debasing loyalty.

Is that not the psychological profile of an Internet troll?

SPORTS BRING US TOGETHER AS A NATION

A few days before he left office, President Obama welcomed the Chicago Cubs to the White House to congratulate them on their long-awaited world championship. Such upbeat media ceremonies were a regular feature of his administration. Obama looked to sports as a refuge from the burdens of his office, while public expressions of fandom became a dependable means of connecting to citizens, men in particular, who might resent his policies, his erudition, and/or his race.

Obama used his final public appearance as president to make a more striking argument: that sports played a role in the nation's moral progress. "It is worth remembering—because sometimes people wonder, 'Well, why are you spending time on sports? There's other stuff going on'—throughout our history, sports has had this power to bring us together, even when the country is divided," he insisted. "Sports has changed attitudes and culture in ways that seem subtle but that ultimately made us think differently about ourselves and who we were. It is a game, and it is celebration, but there's a direct line between Jackie Robinson and me standing here." He went on, "Sports has a way, sometimes, of changing hearts in a way that politics or business doesn't. And sometimes it's just a matter of us being able to escape and relax from the difficulties of our days, but sometimes it also speaks to something better in us."

I've been a fan my entire life, and written at length about the role of sports in American culture. I agree that there are moments when our worship of athletic heroism overpowers our prejudice. But Obama is telling a bad story when it comes to sports, trafficking in delusions that are almost never confronted in this country.

To the extent that white Americans accepted Jackie Robinson, for instance, they did so because of his physical prowess, not the content of his character. Ditto Jesse Owens and Michael Jordan and Serena Williams. The reason athletes matter to us, the reason they get paid millions and get to visit the White House, the reason they *appear* exempt from bigotry, is because they are very good at playing games we like to watch.

Given the history of African Americans in this country, and the reasons for which they've been esteemed by whites, Obama's argument that sports make us think "differently about ourselves" is laughable. Take a gander at the NFL combine, where young men, most of them African Americans from poor backgrounds, are measured and prodded and put through their paces for the benefit of white owners.

I say all this as a devout and frankly tortured fan. If we're going to credit the arena for the virtues it instills—teamwork, discipline, sacrifice, poise—we should also be honest about sport's essential value system. For all its grace and drama, sports boils down to a binary fueled by two incentives: winning and money.

To become a fan is to partake in a subtle but pervasive form of indoctrination, a style of thought that instinctively privileges competition over cooperation, aggression over empathy, tribal allegiance over communalism. Obama can indulge in the mythos of sports all he wants. But much of the reason his legacy is being torn asunder is because a fan mentality now dominates our civic culture.

♦ ♦ ♦

I return to Postman: "We do not measure a culture by its output of undisguised trivialities but by what it claims as significant."

When ESPN first came on the air in 1979, a network devoted entirely to sports sounded nuts. Today, a quarter of the channels in any given cable package are devoted to sports.

Coverage has extended from the games themselves to a vast collateral realm of highlights and hype that fuels thousands of radio shows, websites, and podcasts. Sports represents print journalism's lone growth sector.

As Americans have become geographically uprooted and spiritually unmoored, they have turned to fandom as a source of identity, a refuge from the anxieties of adulthood, a common language in a balkanized culture. Our fandom is so all-encompassing that it's almost impossible to detect, like a trace element in the air. The number of hours we spend consuming sports dwarfs the number we devote to reading, volunteer work, exercise, and religious worship.

Sports has reshaped the architecture of our major cities, funneled public monies into the pockets of billionaire owners, and created an economic model that privileges low-wage seasonal jobs over sustainable economic growth. It has infiltrated our educational system so thoroughly that we think nothing of our tax dollars subsidizing stadiums and famous coaches rather than teachers and textbooks. It has warped our values in ways we barely ever discuss.

◆ ◆ ◆

Back in 1945, George Orwell wrote an essay called "The Sporting Spirit" in which he warned that, "Serious sport has nothing to do with fair play. It is bound up with hatred, jealousy, boastfulness, disregard of all rules and sadistic pleasure in witnessing violence: in other words, it is war minus the shooting."

As a fan, I bristled a bit at this assessment. But I thought, too, of Trump's curious cameo some years ago as a professional wrestler. Cast as an adiposal avenger, Trump rushes the ring in a three-piece suit, assaults an unctuous corporate villain with a chair, then shaves his head in the middle of the ring. That's not the exact story of the 2016 campaign, but it's not a bad approximation.

Trump was successful in part because there is a powerful part of our brains that lusts after this kind of adrenal jolt, what I think of as the *sports brain*. The sports brain has no interest in the busy work of our critical faculties or conscience. It doesn't give a hoot about governance or empathy or ethics. The other campaigns wanted to stage an election. Trump made it a fight.

◆ ◆ ◆

Trump's central perspective on sports has been that of an owner: he sees a profit source, from the betting books of his casinos to his ill-fated purchase of a United States Football League franchise to his gilded golf courses.

But he also knows how to rouse a crowd using the language of fandom. His rhetoric has none of the inspirational notes struck by Obama. Sports isn't about breaking down barriers of prejudice but regressing to our primal selves, celebrating the vicious instincts that dwell inside all of us.

Early in his campaign, the candidate spoke to a crowd in Reno, Nevada, about our invasion of Iraq. His basic point was that the United States and its stupid weak leaders hadn't been man enough to convert that sovereign country into our own private gas pump. But as often happens, Trump stumbled upon an even more galling subject—the feminization of the NFL:

It's a Sunday, who the hell wants to watch these crummy games? I just want to watch the end. By the way—okay, let me go there for a second . . . so I'm watching a game yesterday. What used to be considered a great tackle, a violent head-on [tackle], a violent—if that was done by Dick Butkus, they'd say he's the greatest player. If that were done by Lawrence Taylor—it was done by Lawrence Taylor and Dick Butkus and Ray Nitschke, right? Ray Nitschke—you used to see these tackles and it was incredible to watch, right? Now they tackle. 'Oh, head-on-head collision, 15 yards!' The whole game is all screwed up. You say, 'Wow, what a tackle.' Bing. Flag. Football has become soft. Football has become soft. Now, I'll be criticized for that. They'll say, 'Oh, isn't that terrible.' But football has become soft like our country has become soft.

Trump's animating theme here is masculine doubt—more specifically, lost virility—a personal preoccupation that reflexively attaches itself to his larger conception of American identity. But the specific game Trump was referencing matters. It was a playoff contest between the Pittsburgh Steelers and the Cincinnati Bengals, which turned on a particular play. Steelers receiver Antonio Brown leapt high for a pass. Unable to snag the ball, he sailed defenseless through the air. Bengals linebacker Vontaze Burfict launched himself at Brown and smashed his head with such violence that Brown appeared concussed before he hit the ground. Replays of the hit showed his head flailing, his body limp and contorted. "Oh my goodness," one of the announcers said, as Brown lay motionless on the ground.

When Trump talked about the NFL going soft, he was arguing that football should have *more* hits like this, and that any attempt to curb this sort of brutality represented an assault not just on the integrity of the game but on the American spirit itself. *Nobody wants to hurt each other anymore.* This was his lament on the campaign trail. "Protestors—they realize there are no consequences to protesting anymore. There used to be consequences. There are none anymore."

Trump has been consistent in advancing this worldview. You can draw a straight line from his father's exhortation that he become "a killer" to Roy Cohn's mentorship to his call for the execution of the Central Park Five to his routine courting of battery against protestors at his rallies. America thrives when there are no referees throwing sissy flags, when its leaders are strong enough to punish dissent, when the infliction of pain upon your foe isn't just necessary but heroic.

Here was Trump's reaction to the news that two young men had cited him as the inspiration for beating a homeless Mexican man with a metal pole: "I will say that people who are following me are very passionate. They love this country, and they want this country to be great again."

◆ ◆ ◆

By this rather narrow formulation, America would be best to set its cultural clock back to the Fifties. But the deeper yearning here is to return to an era that pre-dates the Enlightenment, with its constricting laws of reason and science. The sports brain is a throwback to Hobbes, and the idea that any successful government must be strong enough to counteract the "state of nature" in which men will always battle one another—whether for scarce resources or honor—in a "war of all against all." It is worth noting that Hobbes was writing in the 1600s, in the midst of a grewsome civil war, and that he argued for rule by an absolute sovereign.

The American political model, though conceived amid the abomination of slavery, sets out a much more sanguine vision, one based on compromise, comity, and a balance of powers. The Founders recognized that political leaders would prescribe different remedies to common crises, but that they would need to work together to serve the people.

Trumpism is predicated on the zero-sum model; in order for you to win, the other guy has to lose. He cannot see trade deals as mutually beneficial, for example, because America can win only if other countries are losing. If renewable energy wins, coal country loses. If immigration wins, natives lose. If Islam wins, Christianity loses. This style of thought finds its purest expression in our collective worship of sports, a worship that has intensified in direct correlation to the anxieties of late-model capitalism.

To put it more plainly: we, as a people, have become pathologically competitive. Has there ever been another nation so eager to present human endeavor as sport? We have turned everything into a competition: dating, cooking, singing, dancing, scavenging, traveling, even courtship.

Trump merely reflects the political iteration of this mindset. While his opponents droned on about policies, he extolled his personal fortune and poll numbers and crowd sizes. He wasn't trying to explain *why* he deserved the presidency, because the goal was victory not governance. By the inborn logic of the sports brain, victory would *amount* to governance. Trump would banish the "losers" from Washington and magically usher in an era of "winning." Serving as president has shattered this conception of the office and exposed his ineptitude. Trump has responded by repeatedly citing his Electoral College victory.

Easy as this mindset is to mock, Americans all across the political spectrum got caught in the same loop. How much time did we spend checking the polls and the predictive models at 538 or the *New York Times* Upshot as the election drew close? How many stories did we consume about who was ahead and by how much, about strategy and play-calling? Is it any wonder, then, that the media spent so much time focused on the scoreboard, and not the stakes?

We should all be horrified at the post-election study, conducted by Harvard's Shorenstein Center, which revealed that just ten percent of the 2016 election coverage focused on policy. But we should also understand that this dismal statistic redounds to us.

♦ ♦ ♦

A decade ago, I began drafting a novel that arose from my unfortunate addiction to sports talk radio during the Bush regime. My hero was the host of an overnight show for a failing station outside Boston. The book was my rather ham-handed attempt to portray how fandom had colonized American thought, how it agitated our violent spirit, our racial animus, and our rampant entitlement. As a guilt-stricken fan, I was trying to understand why so many Americans had traded in the duties of citizenship for the pleasures of fandom, how we could be so passionate about our teams and so indifferent to our political circumstance.

My theory was that sports awakened us, spiritually, from the cynical fugue of modern life by providing an authentic sense of beauty and heroism in a sea of artifice. "Maybe there was something childish about the whole enterprise," my hero thinks, "but at least it was real, not the endless bullshit of the non-sporting world, the tamed aggressions of the modern office, the nonstop ad campaign that passed for a national culture—sports was the opposite of all that, a dangerous improvisation."

That's what fans would come to see in Trump, a danger-ous improvisation. And it's why so many of them seemed genuinely confused by the anguish his triumph generated. To them, the election was nothing more than a rousing upset, proof that a brash political rookie could take down a waning veteran. They gave no deeper thought to the consequences.

It's useful here to recall the poet Juvenal, who scolded the people of Rome for abdicating their civic duties and instead bowing to the distraction of "bread and circuses." He, too, saw the public appetite for athletic spectacle as a symptom of Rome's unseriousness. The Republic he condemned devolved into an autocracy.

Americans are less inclined to link our passion for sports to our political dysfunction. But the connection is far more profound than the one Juvenal lamented. Because watching sports doesn't just distract us from politics. It shapes the manner in which we think and behave politically.

Orwell connected the dots 70 years ago. After the fall of Rome, sports faded in prominence—until the 19th century. "Then, chiefly in England and the United States, games were built up into a heavily-financed activity, capable of attracting vast crowds and rousing savage passions. . . . Games are taken seriously in London and New York, and they were taken seriously in Rome and Byzantium: in the Middle Ages they were played, and probably played with much physical brutality, but they were not mixed up with politics nor a cause of group hatreds."

So what changed? "There cannot be much doubt that the whole thing is bound up with the rise of nationalism—that is, with the lunatic modern habit of identifying oneself with large power units and seeing everything in terms of competitive prestige." Trumpism represented that large power unit, something fans could plug into, like a football team, which would go out and kick ass on their behalf.

♦ ♦ ♦

Remember that study documenting the rise of "hyper-partisanship"? It noted that, as recently as the 1980s, Americans took a neutral view of opposing partisans, and accepted them as well-intentioned. It also found that our current ingrained feelings of hostility for the opposing party have almost nothing to do with ideology or policy. This was basically social scientists quantifying the sports brain.

Anyone who has ever rooted for a team recognizes the mindset. No matter what your team does, you find a way to justify your loyalty. No matter what the rival team does, you find a way to demonize them. It's that simple. Fandom turns our moral codes as floppy as felt pennants. Nobody likes a dirty player on the other team. But everyone wants one on their own.

Our allegiance may take root in geographic or familial loyalty. It may be enhanced by admiration for particular athletes, or a style of play. But fandom is ultimately a religious arrangement, a covenant based on a powerful and irrational identification. Fans live in a state of helplessness in which their sole locus of control is the object and ardor of their devotion. This is precisely how most Americans feel about their political system. Citizens who have spent decades rooting for laundry aren't looking to parse the efficacy or ethics of policy matters. They pull for their candidates to win by any means necessary. Thus, Trump was able to consolidate GOP support faster than Mitt Romney, despite the fact that many of his positions repudiated party orthodoxy, and that many Republicans distrusted him.

But the sports brain was even more powerful this election cycle, because there was a third team involved: the Russian operatives who hacked emails and spread disinformation about Clinton at the behest of Vladimir Putin. It should surprise no one that the Trump campaign played ball with Putin, or that they lied about this collusion for months. The reaction of other Republicans is more chilling. How did they respond to the news that a murderous despot was interfering with our free elections? They did not. Because the Russians were helping their team.

◆ ◆ ◆

I can remember waking up on the morning after the Reagan/ Mondale election of 1984. I was a freshman in college, appropriately bereaved, and wandering down my dorm hall when I saw a large, bearish figure in shower sandals lumbering toward me. This was Sam Burkholdt, the hall's resident hockey player. "We kicked your ass," Sam boomed. "Your guy got three points! Three lousy points!"

Mondale actually received thirteen electoral votes. But as a fellow jock I wasn't about to quibble. I understood the prerogatives of an ass whooping. I didn't even blame Sam. He was an insecure kid born into wealth, a loudmouth and a bully who was responding to the election night coverage, which, with its giant scoreboard and color-coded map, looked more like a sports broadcast than anything else.

Americans have always, to some extent, chosen to regard politics as sport. What's changed is that our media and political classes now function to intensify this bad story. Rather than interviewing experts who might illuminate policy, cable news outlets stage pundit cage matches. Candidate debates are no longer forums to showcase competing ideas. They are promoted and analyzed like prizefights. Who won? Were there any knockout blows?

When Mitch McConnell announced in 2009 that the GOP's top priority would be to make Obama a one-term president, he was acceding to the reality that his voters now function as sports fans. When the enduring image of your national convention—and its unifying message—is an entire arena chanting "Lock her up!" are you staging a political event or a sports rally?

Obama entered office seeking to change Washington's political culture, hoping he would win points for equanimity and respect. Obama lauded sports, but he never managed to get his head around the sports brain, nor the cycle of escalating recrimination and intransigence it initiated. He took a technocratic approach to policy, courted consensus, and avoided conflict. He hoped the presidency would place him above the fray.

Trump understood the fray was all. What he discovered over the course of the campaign was a media willing to render politics as sport, and an electorate willing to endorse his vision of democracy as a zero-sum game.

He won some cheers bashing the NFL. But if Trump had even a particle of common sense, he would have recognized that the league's ascendance foretold his own. For years, fans had been training themselves to compartmentalize, to ignore the corruptions of the game so they could enjoy the spectacle. A football game is dense with strategy and marked by moments of transcendent grace. But it has no moral philosophy beyond an improvised whim to vanquish the opponent. This is the sports brain making sense of the modern world. It is now in the White House, making our national policy.

AMERICAN WOMEN WILL NEVER
EMPOWER A SEXUAL PREDATOR

On the night after the election, I led a writing workshop. The intended subject, absurdly, was How to Write Sex Scenes, which I figured would be a reprieve from the psychic weight of the election. But Trump's victory, and the distress I assumed it would stir within the sort of person who enrolls in a writing workshop, led me to settle on a more appropriate subject: the artistic uses of wrath.

Midway through class, I asked the students to write about a moment of rage in their lives. The most striking response came from a woman I'll call Rachel. She recounted an episode in which she arrived at college, still reeling from the divorce of her parents. A glamorous older classmate sensed her insecurity and took advantage of her in a manner that sounded, at the very least, coercive. He then told a buddy, who mocked her about this liaison in front of a large group. Nearly three decades later, merely uttering the name of the young man who had humiliated her brought a flush to Rachel's cheeks.

After class, I found myself talking with Rachel and another student when, apropos of nothing, she made this declaration: "The one I've never cared for is Michelle Obama."

I'd made several references in class to the seductive power of Trump's rage. But I should emphasize that our post-class chat had not been about the election. Indeed, Rachel's comment seemed to arise from some private conversation she was conducting in her head.

"Michelle Obama?" I said, rather confused. "What did she do?"

"It's her whole approach. I don't want my First Lady showing her arms in public."

I paused, troubled by Rachel's use of the possessive pronoun. "Why shouldn't she show her arms?" I said.

"I just—I believe in modesty. I'd like my First Lady to show some modesty."

My mind flashed, for a confusingly erotic moment, to the nude photos of Melania Trump that had leaked during the campaign. But I didn't say anything, because I could sense an argument in the offing. Like most of the students in class, I was still trying to take in the bleak enormity of the election.

But Rachel wasn't done. She went on to criticize President Obama and to express a generalized, if vague, contempt for the status quo. "What is it you're so afraid of when it comes to Trump anyway?" she demanded. It was at this point that the situation came into focus: Rachel had voted for Trump.

◆ ◆ ◆

I don't know that for a fact. I didn't ask, because I didn't want to know.

I want to be careful not to flatten Rachel into a caricature. She had a college degree in literature. She was, from what I could discern, a loving mother whose own daughter was now in college. She had launched a successful business. As I listened to her story in class, I'd admired her insight and courage.

This was what made her comments after class so mystifying. What had happened to *that* woman? Where had she gone?

As absurd and grandiose as this will sound, her disappearance struck me as one of the central mysteries at the heart of the 2016 election—and, to some more obscure degree, the moral erosion of the American experiment. I mean by this that some essential synapse within Rachel had corroded. She could no longer draw a connection between the trauma she had described an hour earlier and the ascension of a man who routinely and publicly humiliated women, and who bragged about sexually assaulting them.

◆ ◆ ◆

I've spent more hours than I care to admit replaying this episode in my head, trying to make it add up. How did a candidate who uttered the words *Grab them by the pussy* compel
42 percent of his potential victims to vote for him, including
more than half of the white female voters in America?

I've read hundreds of interviews with female Trump voters setting out their rationale: business acumen, mistrust of
Hillary, resentment of immigrants, etc. There's almost never any specific citation of policy, but that's not surprising.
What all these women had in common was a willingness
to dismiss or tolerate his words and behaviors and attitudes
toward other women.

Trump didn't just drag misogyny out of the shadows;
he cast it in neon, touting his endowment and his stamina,
demonstrating his dominion over women. His private conduct was merely an extension of what we saw in public as
he stalked Clinton or lashed out at uppity female anchors.
But Trumpism activated something more visceral: the hidden power of ingrained patriarchal thought. The most potent
weapon in the Trump arsenal wasn't virility, but feminine
complicity.

It took me a few weeks to get it through my skull, but
Rachel was trying to teach me something about the nature
of trauma: that sometimes it's psychologically safer to enable
the abuser than to acknowledge the abuse.

Of all the students in that workshop, Rachel was probably the one who knew best the pain caused by men who believe they *can do anything* to women. The story she told in class had awakened that vulnerability. This is precisely why she had felt it necessary to issue her belligerent challenge after class: *What is it you're so afraid of when it comes to Trump?*

She wasn't talking to me. She was talking to herself.

◆ ◆ ◆

A few days before the election, I was invited to give a brief presentation at a conference on female empowerment. At the opening night party, I sat down next to a fellow speaker who turned out to be the vice president in charge of hiring at a major entertainment media company in the Bay Area.

I immediately asked her about the election because I wanted to hear what a female executive in charge of hiring had to say about the unprecedented and extreme gender dynamics of the race.

"I don't trust Hillary, if that's what you mean," the woman replied curtly. "She's too corrupt. Her email server. The Clinton Foundation. Benghazi."

So much for my smug liberal assumptions.

When I asked about Trump, my interlocutor said this: "I'm not crazy about him either. But at least he never laughed at a rape victim."

"A *rape* victim?" I said, somewhat dazedly.

"Yeah, she defended a rapist and got him acquitted then she laughed at the victim. There's a tape of the whole thing."

I had only a hazy recollection of Trump lobbing this accusation, as a frantic effort to deflect attention from his pussy grabbing outburst. So later that night I went online to find the story about Hillary Clinton and the rape victim. Clinton *had* defended a rapist, some 40 years ago, after a judge ordered her to take the case. Her client wasn't acquitted. He was ruled guilty and accepted a plea bargain, under pressure from the victim's mother.

There was audio of Clinton discussing the case years later with a journalist. She did snicker a few times, recalling the troubling events. But this laughter was plainly directed at the incompetence of the prosecution, whom she felt had mishandled the case. She never discussed the victim or laughed at her. Her basic assessment was that the criminal justice system had failed the victim. None of this was a matter of opinion.

My mind kept circling back to the VP at the party. I imagined two job candidates walking into her office. The first was a verbally belligerent male with no experience and a documented record of bigoted statements, racial discrimination, bankruptcy, fraud, multiple allegations of sexual harassment, a man who bragged, while at work and on tape, of sexually assaulting women. The second was an ambitious woman with vast experience who had been accused of corruption repeatedly, without evidence. This executive had breezily announced to me, on the eve of the hire date, that she saw no difference between the two.

I understood why so many men resented Hillary Clinton, how she became a psychic punching bag for men bedeviled by self-doubt and angry, in particular, at ambitious women in the workplace. What I didn't get was why a woman specifically focused on female professional empowerment—as signaled by speaking at a huge conference *about the need for female professional empowerment*—would treat Clinton and Trump as moral equivalents.

Maybe the VP wanted to see her industry deregulated, or her tax bill cut. Maybe she was raised a loyal Republican, or believed abortion was murder. I'd never know her political motives. But her underlying psychic strategy was painfully apparent. The only way she could dismiss the behaviors of a self-professed sexual predator was to accept, with no effort at verification, a libelous fantasy in which Clinton used her professional power to protect a rapist and sadistically shame his girl victim. She projected her outlandish complicity onto Clinton.

♦ ♦ ♦

Every woman who supported Trump had to find ways to contend with these feelings, whether or not they cared to acknowledge them. I thought about the ways in which abuse often operates within a family system, how the sins of the father get displaced onto the women who threaten him. And this led me back to a series of in-depth articles I'd written in Miami, about a Cuban-American family in which a teenage daughter accused her stepfather of sexual abuse and the state took custody of her and six younger siblings.

Police spent months investigating and concluded that there was no evidence of abuse. The accuser herself renounced her claims. My pieces focused on the plight of the parents, both physicians, who had been denied access to their children for years. Eventually, a juvenile court judge held an evidentiary hearing and ordered the family reunited. Prosecutors initiated a criminal investigation of the social workers in the case. Justice served.

And then one day an anonymous envelope showed up in my mailbox at work, with a cassette inside. It was immediately (and nauseatingly) clear to me that the voices on the tape belonged to the stepfather and his teenage accuser. She had secretly recorded a recent car trip. "I can't wait to have sex," the stepfather announced, after some banter. "I'm talking about a good-time fuck." The girl's infant son, also somewhere in that car, could be heard throughout the recording.

Looking back, what I find most remarkable about this saga is how the women in the family conspired to cover up the stepfather's sins. Rather than banding together to cast out the abuser, the mother and her two eldest daughters became sworn enemies. Not even the tape of the stepfather's sexual advances—eventually made public—changed this dynamic. He insisted it was fake, and his wife believed him. She was a powerful woman, a prominent neurologist. But her need to protect herself from the monstrous implications of his sins turned her into a monster.

◆ ◆ ◆

I keep thinking, too, of a strange episode from my years as a reporter down in El Paso. I was profiling an aging cattleman and spent a week on his West Texas ranch, stumbling around in my wingtips. The rancher was gelding his herd and he had a bunch of local teenagers working for him. They ran the steer into chutes and locked them in place while the old man castrated them with a scalpel, then cauterized the wound with a branding iron.

The smell of the burnt flesh and the shuddering of the animals turned my stomach, but I pretended it was no big deal. I wanted to be accepted by these young guys, to somehow ingratiate myself to them, or at least get one of them to grant me an interview. I hovered around as they ate lunch, and affected a drawl borrowed from every country music song I'd ever heard. They wanted nothing to do with me, naturally. They could tell I hailed from some place they would never visit willingly, where guys in vintage bowling shirts got paid for asking stupid questions.

On my last day, one of the young guys unexpectedly called out to me. "Hey, reporter man," he said. It was maybe 90 degrees and they were sitting in the shade of a mesquite, sipping cans of Pepsi. One of his comrades got up and began sauntering toward me.

The ranch hand walked right up to me. He was taller than the rest, with soft round cheeks. "Got you something," he said, in a husky tenor. He extended a cupped hand and gestured for me to do the same.

Oh my, I thought, *a gift.*

I looked into his eyes, hoping to convey my gratitude, and realized, with a start, that this young guy was, in fact, a young woman, her dirty blond hair tucked up into her Stetson. Her face flickered with a bashful misery as she set a warm, slippery egg-shaped thing into my hand.

I glanced down at the bull testicle, the pale blue membrane threaded with veins, the blood brushed from her palm onto mine, and together we listened to the snickering of the ranch hands behind her. I could see that she'd been enlisted to carry out this ruse because she was an interloper, too, trying to negotiate a world ruled by men and she had figured out that the best way to do so, maybe the only way, was to ape the cruelty of this realm, to pass her shame along to someone even more vulnerable.

Crazy as this will sound, I now see this scene as Trump-ism in vitro, the cruel gift bestowed upon us wimpy city slickers by rustic America, the prank engineered by smirking men but carried out by women who felt they had no choice.

BAD STORY #12

OUR COURT JESTERS WILL
RESCUE THE KINGDOM

I n January of 2016, on the eve of his final State of the Union
address, President Obama welcomed NBC's Matt Lauer to
the White House for one of those awkward walk-and-talk interviews that culminates with a manly handshake in the Oval
Office. After a few warm-up questions, Lauer mentioned the
GOP frontrunner. Wasn't his stunning rise proof that Americans were more divided than ever?

"Talk to me if he wins," Obama said. "But I feel confident
that the overwhelming majority of Americans are looking for
the kind of politics that does feed our hopes and not our fears."

Lauer pressed on. "So when you stand and deliver that
State of the Union address, in no part of your mind and brain
can you imagine Donald Trump standing up one day and
delivering the State of the Union address?"

Obama sniggered. "Well, I can imagine it in a 'Saturday
Night' skit."

What's most telling here is the direction Obama's mind travels when asked to confront the possibility of Trump's election: he goes to the world of parody—a place that is inherently unserious.

♦ ♦ ♦

Here's the crazy part: Obama kept doubling down. A few weeks before the election, he went on *Jimmy Kimmel Live!* to perform a routine in which he read insulting tweets on his phone. The final one came as no surprise. "President Obama will go down as perhaps the worst president in the history of the United States! @realDonaldTrump." Obama waited a beat before delivering his riposte: "Well, @realDonaldTrump, at least I will go *down* as a president." Then he held out his phone and let it fall, like a rapper dropping the mic.

To the tens of millions of citizens who saw this clip Obama was saying, quite explicitly: *It's okay to laugh at Trump, because he's never going to win.*

Can we speculate as to the potential effect of this bit? Not to cable junkies or partisans, but to that much larger bloc of voters who had heard some bad things about Trump, who harbored an inchoate feeling of concern or mistrust, but who remained unsure as to whether, amid the many competing duties and distractions of a Tuesday in November, they would find time to cast a ballot? Can we assume some percentage of the roughly 103 million registered voters who chose *not* to cast a ballot might have been swayed by stories suggesting that doing so was meaningless? Let's say that was true of just one percent of non-voters. That's more than a million votes, in an election decided by 79,000 votes across three swing states.

To drill down a bit more: two million fewer African Americans turned out for Clinton than for Obama in 2012. In Michigan, she received 300,000 fewer votes than Obama and lost by 10,000. In Wisconsin, she received 230,000 fewer votes than Obama and lost by 22,000. Many factors contributed to these declines: Obama's greater popularity, the Clinton campaign's blunders, voter suppression efforts, and the ugly tenor of the campaign, which caused plenty of low-interest voters to tune out. But in a race decided by a margin that equates to .077 percent of the total non-voters, Obama's public dismissal of Trump takes on a much darker cast.

If it seems like I'm piling on Obama here, I would ask you to think again about that Correspondents' Dinner back in 2011, which Trump's confidantes point to as the psychological trigger for his eventual run. The sitting president made a point of inviting a thin-skinned celebrity to this event for the express purpose of mocking him in front of DC's power elite.

The unseriousness of our electorate starts at the top.

◆ ◆ ◆

Neil Postman was wise to all this. *Amusing Ourselves to Death* offers a vision of the future so frighteningly specific as to foresee the president mugging on late-night television. Programs would arise, he predicted, that show "how television recreates and degrades our conceptions of news, political debate, religious thought, etc." These would "take the form of parodies, along the lines of *Saturday Night Live* and *Monty Python*."

That is the world we now inhabit, one in which televised comedians serve as our leading moralists. While the right reacts to the dysfunction of our civic institutions with delusions of persecution and corresponding spasms of sadism, the left indulges in clever sketches that convert our anguish into disposable laughs. These are the two dominant responses to the state of our union: America as a horror movie, basically, or a farce. Don't bother looking for the nuanced drama about a liberal democracy struggling to maintain faith in the mechanisms of self-governance. That one doesn't sell enough popcorn.

◆ ◆ ◆

As host of *The Daily Show*, Jon Stewart was an astute cultural critic with impeccable timing, the courage to call out con artists, and the capacity to educate his audience without coming off as pedantic. Like Twain and Mencken before him, Stewart defended reason and factual accuracy in an age of hypocrisy and hype, and plied the dying art of critical thought. I watched his program, on and off, for several years.

I feel compelled to make these points because, by the time he left *The Daily Show* in 2015, he was widely regarded as a secular prophet who inspired an entire subgenre of satire, from *The Colbert Report* to *Full Frontal with Samantha Bee* to *Last Week Tonight with John Oliver*. And thus anyone who argues that Stewart might represent more troubling aspects of our age is written off as a self-righteous hater who doesn't get that *he's just a comedian.*

For the record, I get that he's just a comedian. The question is why, in the decade leading up to the 2016 election, Stewart went from being "just a comedian" to "the most trusted man in America" in the words of the *New York Times*?

Here's my take: a majority of our citizens, of every ideological persuasion, share the same disquieting suspicion: that we are powerless to fix our broken institutions. For some, religion remains a source of salvation. Others place their trust in the bluster of demagogues, or simply chose to live in a fog of frantic material and athletic distraction.

The rest of us—the Troubled but Tame Majority, let's say—chose to embrace Stewart as our spirit guide. Because he was the one public figure capable of articulating the depth of our dysfunction without totally bumming us out. He converted our despair, instead, into laughter. But something more insidious was happening in the process. We were learning to see politics and media as a joke.

There were notable exceptions to this pattern. Stewart was able to help push through a health care measure for first responders to 9/11, for instance. He exposed various charlatans. He even ventured into the larger media ecosystem to have his say, most famously when he lectured the hosts of CNN's debate show, *Crossfire*. "Stop, stop, stop, stop hurting America," Stewart told Tucker Carlson. "See, the thing is, we need your help. Right now, you're helping the politicians and the corporations. And we're left out there to mow our lawns."

This rant helped enshrine Stewart as a folk hero. The queasy irony of this exchange was that Stewart had devoted hours to mocking *Crossfire*. If he was a humble populist raging against dysfunction, he was also a parasite of that dysfunction. His job depended on blowhards such as Carlson.

In an adoring *Times* profile he spoke of his comedic mission as though it were an upscale anti-depressant. "It's a wonderful feeling to have this toxin in your body in the morning, that little cup of sadness, and feel by 7 or 7:30 that night, you've released it in sweat equity and can move on to the next day."

But what if Stewart's daily doses were masking vital symptoms? What if the underlying disease—the one killing American democracy—was unseriousness?

◆ ◆ ◆

Surveying the defects of American governance more than eight decades ago, H.L. Mencken issued the following decree: "The only way that democracy can be made bearable is by developing and cherishing a class of men sufficiently honest and disinterested to challenge the prevailing quacks."

To many of their fans, Stewart and Stephen Colbert represented just such a class. And hope for their leadership was never more keenly felt than in the weeks leading up to their Rally to Restore Sanity and/or Fear. The gathering, a hastily conceived send-up of Glenn Beck's Restoring Honor Rally, took place three days before the 2010 midterm elections.

The event amounted to a goofy variety show, capped by one of Stewart's earnest homilies. Americans are a decent people, he insisted, capable of making "reasonable compromises." As proof, he showed a video of cars merging in the Holland Tunnel. "'Oh my God, is that an NRA sticker on your car, is that an Obama sticker on your car? Well, that's okay. You go and then I'll go.' Sure, at some point there will be a selfish jerk who zips up the shoulder and cuts in at the last minute. But that individual is rare and he is scorned, and not hired as a [TV] analyst."

Almost everything about this riff was baloney. His sidekick Colbert was living proof that networks hire so many selfish jerks as to create a cottage industry of parodic jerks.

The maestros of conservative talk radio, an industry born of commuter rage, had, in fact, taken possession of the Republican Party, with aims on our national discourse.

In Stewart's formulation, the problem wasn't us noble citizens. It was villainous pundits and politicians. But we were the ones who watched those pundits and elected those politicians. Stewart and Colbert made their nut by catering to us Troubled but Tame folks who chose to giggle at the results rather than working to change them.

His closing statement at the rally was anodyne to the point of anti-activism. "If you want to know why I'm here and what I want from you," he declared, "I can only assure you this: you have already given it to me. Your presence was what I wanted." Stewart had convinced more than 200,000 Americans to crowd the National Mall on the eve of a pivotal election, with millions more watching at home. To what end had he mobilized these citizens? Voter registration? Phone banking? Door-to-door canvassing? No, self-congratulation.

Four days later, Tea Party candidates stormed into the House of Representatives, ushering in an era of ideological extremism, congressional gerrymandering, and perpetual gridlock.

Far from challenging the quacks, Stewart and Colbert proved to be invaluable allies. Their shows insulated viewers from feelings of distress that were an appropriate and necessary response to our historical moment.

If I seem harsh here, it's because Stewart and Colbert were clearly smart enough to see their role in the larger scheme. They knew why our political discourse had grown so vicious, and why it had drifted away from matters of policy and moral consequence. It wasn't because of some misunderstanding between cultural factions. It was the desired result of a sustained campaign waged by corporations, lobbyists, politicians, and demagogues—all of whom stood to profit handsomely by the erosion of those civic institutions that might curb their influence. What they needed was a population willing to laugh off this moral depravity, and a few high-tech jesters willing to generate those laughs.

◆ ◆ ◆

One of the few public figures to criticize the Stewart/Colbert rally was Bill Maher, who noted that the hosts had drawn a disgraceful equivalence between the concerted fear mongering of the right and the activism of the left. "Martin Luther King spoke on that mall in the capitol, and he didn't say, 'Remember folks, those Southern sheriffs with the fire hoses and the German shepherds, they have a point too!' No, he said, 'I have a dream. They have a nightmare!'"

But Maher's complaint obscured his own role in the larger process by which the politics of the left has been subsumed by show business. Back in 1993, six years before Stewart took the helm of *The Daily Show*, Maher launched a talk show called *Politically Incorrect* that featured comedians, politicians, and celebrities bantering about politics. The format was popular enough to leap from Comedy Central to ABC to HBO, and—perhaps as telling—to relocate from New York to Los Angeles, where it was easier to book movie stars onto the show.

The central effect of his show wasn't to bring serious political discourse into primetime. It was to recast political discourse as an amusement, an ill-informed squabble filmed before a live studio audience. *Politically Incorrect* was an early breeding ground for a strain of punditry that combined cheesecake glamour with smirking sophistry. Maher provided a platform, and extensive media training, for a series of leggy propagandists who would graduate to roles of prominence in the conservative media. "I think we're the show that kind of made Ann Coulter and Kellyanne [Conway] and Laura Ingraham—you know, those were, like, our blond Republican ladies," he told the *New Yorker*.

Those who saw Maher interview Conway, six weeks before the election, witnessed a noxious example of how the game works. Conway, a Republican pollster who once considered Trump unfit for the presidency, was now his campaign manager and most mendacious defender.

How did Maher treat Conway? Like a fond mentor. "On the one hand, you're enabling pure evil," he quipped. "On the other hand, I'm, like, so proud of you! You started here. You were just a child star on our show."

Conway thanked Maher for "giving me a platform for all those swing voters who watch your show" and proceeded to spin for twelve straight minutes.

"You're so good at what you do," Maher gushed at one point. "So good. I'm just verklempt."

That's how deep the con runs here. Maher styles himself a kind of liberal watchdog for his audience. But his smug tribalism doesn't advance a progressive agenda. It's not meant to. That central goal of his sparring session with Conway was to generate ratings.

◆ ◆ ◆

It's easy to criticize the commercial impulses here, and harder to confront the psychic forces that drive us to seek refuge in Maher, Stewart, et al.

I think here of David Foster Wallace. "What one feels when [politicians] loom into view is just an overwhelming lack of interest," he observed, back in 2000, "the sort of deep disengagement that is often a defense against pain. Against sadness. In fact, the likeliest reason why so many of us care so little about politics is that modern politicians make us sad, hurt us deep down in ways that are hard even to name, much less talk about."

Our programmed defense against such vulnerability is irony. The political satire of the left—though instigated by a genuine desire to call out abuses of power—allowed us to pretend that none of this mattered. Our addiction to these programs became a cheap and reliable opiate for progressive angst. By laughing at democracy's dysfunction, by refusing to take it seriously, we laid the foundation for Trumpism. And when it arrived, we could only soothe our horror by retreating into an endless loop of clips, as if watching Trump derided on *Saturday Night Live* would derail his candidacy.

◆ ◆ ◆

It was inevitable that pundits would respond to Trump's nomination by pleading with Jon Stewart to come out of retirement. Some fantasized that he would succeed where the Fourth Estate had failed, by compelling the electorate to recognize Trump for what he was.

This was certainly wishful thinking. But it also betrayed a basic misunderstanding of the role Stewart had played in our larger cultural saga. Throughout his tenure at *The Daily Show*, Stewart hammered one basic note: that our political and media establishments were feeble and corrupt. Trump hit the same note at every one of his rallies. It was the most convincing aspect of his appeal.

If Stewart's mission was to decant the anguish and rage of the left into laughs, Trump fanned those same emotions into raw political power. Both, in this sense, profited by a loss of faith.

One of the last shows Stewart hosted, in the summer of 2015, aired just hours after Trump announced that he would run for president. Stewart began by muttering a pro forma speech about the sanctity of our electoral process. "But fuck," he declared. "This guy is so much fun!" This led to a flurry of Trump clips. Stewart kept trying to turn his attention "back to the process." But the other candidates were so *boring*. Watching this riff, I couldn't help but to think of the central question raised by Postman: "To whom do we complain . . . when serious discourse dissolves into giggles? What is the antidote to a culture's being drained by laughter?"

I recalled, too, a line Foster Wallace had written about insurgent candidates, how they stirred "a very modern and American type of ambivalence, a sort of interior war between your deep need to believe and your deep belief that the need to believe is bullshit, that there's nothing left anywhere but sales and salesman."

One of the many candidates Stewart dismissed was Bernie Sanders, whose stunning challenge to Hillary Clinton represented, in many ways, a more significant insurgency than Trump's. Sanders wanted a national single-payer health care system. He wanted to impose a tax increase on the affluent and make college tuition free. He'd drawn huge crowds by bluntly articulating the tolls of income inequality.

Sanders was useless to Stewart because he couldn't be reduced to shtick. And Stewart's bottom-line product was shtick. So he ignored the Sanders Revolution and promoted the Trump Follies. Those of us chuckling at home were thereby bonded to Stewart in the great loop of impotence. But burying our pain beneath laughter, year after year, came with a risk few recognized until 2016.

Trump won the GOP nomination, then the presidency, because he activated this "deep need to believe." His cartoonish view of an America in ruins, besieged by dark hordes—the nightmare he'd hustled for decades—felt real to millions of voters. They were primed for a savior even if some part of them knew their standard bearer was just a salesman.

And what was the left's conditioned response?

But fuck, this guy is so much fun.

THERE IS NO SUCH THING AS
FAIR AND BALANCED

B ack in the late nineties, at the tail end of the Clinton era, I was living in the Winter Hill section of Somerville. Once a week, I walked to Star Market for groceries, where I would sometimes spot an elderly woman in a tattered raincoat placing small slips of white paper beneath the wipers of cars in the parking lot. I eventually succumbed to my curiosity and examined one. It warned, in shaky script, that America was on the brink of collapse due to immigrants, liberals, and homosexuals. Those who cared to learn the truth were exhorted to listen to a radio program called *The Savage Nation*, hosted by Michael Savage.

I had listened to *The Savage Nation* a few times, while mired in traffic, and though I did not believe that immigrants and liberals and homosexuals were plotting the demise of our nation—America happened to be enjoying the longest economic expansion in its history—I do remember being struck by the devotion of this woman, who, as a private citizen, had been inspired by Savage to scrawl this warning onto a piece of paper which she then Xeroxed and cut into hundreds of little squares and carried with her to various parking lots in and around Winter Hill.

So who was this Savage?

His real name is Michael Alan Weiner and he was, at that point in his career, a budding talk radio star with an unusual biography. He had worked as a gatekeeper for the psychedelic drug advocate Timothy Leary, and palled around with the Beats in San Francisco, bragging in particular about his relationship with the famous gay poet Allen Ginsberg. He had earned degrees in anthropology, botany, and nutritional ethnomedicine, and dreamed of becoming a stand-up comic in the mold of Lenny Bruce.

By the 1980s, Weiner had become convinced he was being discriminated against in academia because of his race and gender, a sentiment he commemorated in a poem called "The Death of the White Male." He had developed a theory that undocumented workers posed an epidemiological risk to Americans and wrote a book about this, which was rejected by numerous publishers. Rather than give up, Weiner recorded a demo tape full of his rants and sent it out to 250 talk radio stations under the name Michael Savage.

In 1994, Savage landed a fill-in gig at KGO in San Francisco and quickly became the station's most popular host. The slogan he adopted—"To the right of Rush and to the left of God"—suggested the zealous wrath Savage could summon amid his rambling stories. His philosophy, which he called "conservative nationalism," consisted of excoriating Beltway elites and their global conspirators. He advocated the mass murder of Muslims, the mass deportation of immigrants, and a get-tough policy with the "homosexual mafia" and other "vermin."

Savage's equity resided in his ability to paint a vision of America that inflamed the darkest psychological precincts of his listeners. "It's a weak, sick nation," he preached. "A weak, sick, broken nation. And you need men like me to save the country. You need men to stand up and stop crying like a baby over everything . . . No wonder we're being laughed at around the world."

This was the belief system that animated the woman who haunted the parking lots of Winter Hill two decades ago. Those of us living amid the peace and prosperity of Clinton's America looked upon her mission as pitiable and deluded. What world was she living in, anyway?

At that point, *The Savage Nation* was home to 20 million listeners. One of them was named Donald Trump, whom Savage would eventually dub "the Winston Churchill of our time."

◆ ◆ ◆

To understand the full significance of *The Savage Nation* requires a sustained look into the origins of radio in this country. The framers of the Constitution simply never envisioned a technology that could reach an audience of millions instantly. Many lawmakers believed the medium should be non-commercial and government run.

"American thought and American politics will be largely at the mercy of those who operate these stations, for publicity is the most powerful weapon that can be wielded in a republic," Luther Johnson, a Texas legislator, argued in 1926. "And when such a weapon is placed in the hands of one person, or a single selfish group is permitted to either tacitly or otherwise acquire ownership or dominate these broadcasting stations throughout the country, then woe be to those who dare differ with them. It will be impossible to compete with them in reaching the ears of the American people."

Such concerns led Congress to pass the Radio Act of 1927, which established that the government owned the public airwaves, but that it would grant licenses to private companies to use them "if public convenience, interest or necessity will be served thereby."

A decade later, FDR pushed for the creation of the Federal Communications Commission (FCC) to regulate the airwaves. The FCC, "fearing a further commercialized, conservative-biased, and corporate dominated medium," passed the Mayflower Doctrine in 1941, which required broadcasters "to allot a reasonable amount of time to the treatment of controversial issues" and assigned them "an affirmative duty to seek [and] provide representative expression of all responsible shades of opinion." The FCC eventually replaced the Mayflower Doctrine with the Fairness Doctrine, which called for honest programming that afforded "reasonable opportunity for opposing viewpoints."

Opponents immediately painted the Fairness Doctrine as an assault on the First Amendment for allowing the government to exert editorial control. In practice, the Doctrine never required that programs be ideologically balanced, or offer equal time for opposing views. It simply forbid stations from airing a single perspective exclusively. Whether the subject was a national policy debate or a local referendum question, broadcasters had a duty to present viewpoints with which their listeners disagreed. This is why, over the years, groups as diverse as the ACLU and the National Rifle Association endorsed the Fairness Doctrine.

To put this in modern terms: the FCC wanted to make sure that stations didn't become for-profit echo chambers.

◆ ◆ ◆

Consider the case of the only TV station ever to have its license permanently revoked under the Fairness Doctrine: WLBT, the NBC affiliate in Jackson, Mississippi. WLBT's ownership not only supported racial segregation, but openly worked to oppose civil rights with groups such as the White Citizens' Council, which operated a bookstore in the lobby of the station's studios in downtown Jackson. The station provided a platform for those fighting the federal government's efforts to provide African Americans access to voting, public schools, and other basic amenities. This was entirely permissible under the Fairness Doctrine. But the station also censored any views to the contrary.

In 1955, for example, the civil rights lawyer Thurgood Marshall, later named the first African American to the Supreme Court, appeared on the *Today Show*. WLBT refused to air the national feed, posting a sign reading *Sorry, Cable Trouble*. Station Manager Fred Beard explained that he had pulled the interview because NBC had become an instrument of "Negro propaganda." The station routinely suppressed *any* coverage of the Civil Rights movement by feigning technical difficulties. It also refused to air entertainment programs that included African-American actors, or made even mild references to racial justice.

Civil rights groups, along with NBC itself, sent numerous petitions to the FCC, complaining that WLBT's owner, Lamar Broadcasting, was in flagrant violation of the Fairness Doctrine. The FCC ruled, not once, but twice, in favor of Lamar. The only reason Lamar's license was finally revoked, in 1969, was because a federal judge named Warren Burger ordered the FCC to do so.

To summarize: the FCC, though legally required to enforce the Fairness Doctrine, allowed a TV station to blatantly censor its news coverage and to act as a propaganda tool against racial justice and federal law for two decades. Only a legal opinion written by the eventual Chief Justice of the Supreme Court compelled the FCC to start doing its job.

◆ ◆ ◆

Or consider the case of the investigative journalist Fred J. Cook. In 1964, he published a book called *Barry Goldwater: Extremist of the Right*, which infuriated conservatives. A man named Reverend Billy James Hargis used his daily show on a Pennsylvania radio station, *Christian Crusade*, to uncork a slanderous fifteen-minute tirade against Cook.

Cook requested a chance to respond, citing the Fairness Doctrine, which guaranteed citizens the right to respond to such personal attacks, on air. The station refused, citing the First Amendment right to Freedom of the Press. Cook sued. The case wound up in the Supreme Court, which sided, unanimously, with Cook.

The gist of the decision was that the rights of viewers and listeners took precedence over that of private broadcasters. "It is the purpose of the First Amendment to preserve an uninhibited marketplace of ideas in which truth will ultimately prevail," wrote Justice Byron White, "rather than to countenance monopolization of that market, whether it be by the government itself or a private licensee. It is the right of the public to receive suitable access to social, political, esthetic, moral, and other ideas and experiences which is crucial here . . . There is no sanctuary in the First Amendment for unlimited private censorship operating in a medium not open to all."

What you're seeing in these cases is public servants struggling to prevent bad stories—fraudulent, biased, even malicious ones—from polluting our discourse. The Fairness Doctrine required that private broadcasters set aside partisan or profit motives to serve the public interest.

That idea perished with Ronald Reagan. As part of his wider effort to deregulate and privatize, he chose a former broadcast industry lawyer named Mark Fowler to head the FCC. "The perception of broadcasters as community trustees should be replaced by a view of broadcasters as marketplace participants," Fowler argued. TV was "just another appliance—it's a toaster with pictures."

Emboldened by the legal opinion of two little-known judges, Antonin Scalia and Robert Bork, Fowler stopped enforcing the Fairness Doctrine. Station owners quickly ditched public affairs programming and consolidated into monopolies. When Congress voted to reinstate the rule,

Reagan vetoed the bill. In 1987, the FCC abolished the Doctrine. Later, it eliminated two corollary rules, one prohibiting on-air personal attacks, the second preventing broadcasters from endorsing political candidates.

◆ ◆ ◆

It's important to be clear, at this point, about the limits of the Fairness Doctrine. It was never intended as a panacea for the Fourth Estate. In practice, it simply discouraged station owners from hiring controversial hosts, because they feared the legal fallout: the requirement to air opposing opinions, the risk of fines, or a lost license. It was basically a spoiler plate for propaganda.

With the spoiler plate gone, conservative media roared to life. Station owners, some motivated by ideology, most by profit, stacked their schedules with silver-tongued ideologues. The moribund AM radio band came alive with ranters. In 1996, Fox News launched, offering viewers the same partisan formula on the picture toaster. This meant that a citizen could move through his entire day, from car to living room, from speaker to screen, hearing the same aggrieved agitprop.

But why did conservative hosts corner the medium so quickly? As with any market boom, the answer resides in a confluence of factors: a remarkably potent product, effective salesmen, and customers yearning for relief.

It's worth starting with the question of audience. In 1951, the philosopher Hannah Arendt wrote a book called *The Origins of Totalitarianism*, in which she argued that totalitarianism is, in fact, a kind of organized loneliness, one that takes root in societies where people feel angry and dislocated, left behind by capitalist expansion. People who lose this sense of identity and rootedness come to feel superfluous and this makes them frantic to find a "telos," or a grand narrative, that will grant their life meaning and direction.

This is precisely what the most popular talk radio hosts did for listeners, and what inspired their fanatical devotion. They weren't just providing three hours of blarney to banish the boredom of the afternoon commute. They were constructing a coherent and thrilling worldview. The central feature of this worldview was that our traditional institutions could not be trusted. Government was inept when it was not actually malicious and the only reason you didn't hear more about this was because the rest of the media was in on the plot. Whether you realized it or not, *you were in danger every single minute of every day*—in danger of having your constitutional rights assaulted, of being taxed into penury, of being disrespected, dismissed, enslaved, even killed.

Hosts essentially mass marketed the victimology Richard Hofstadter described, aggrandizing the petty symptoms of cultural dislocation experienced by their listeners—older white men, mostly—into riveting epics of paranoia. While

NPR brewed its weak tea of passive reporting, talk radio slung espresso shots of rhapsodic gaslighting. For years, I harbored a secret conservative talk habit and, if I'm being honest, a grudging admiration for its practitioners. This should explain my decision to write not one, but two, novels about talk radio hosts.

In a literary sense, they understood the concept of stakes, that listeners hungered for a sense of heroic urgency, what Virginia Woolf called "the strange human craving for the pleasure of feeling afraid." Did Limbaugh and his comrades traffic in lies and innuendo? Sure. But ask any novelist what matters more: that you misled your readers, or that you brought them alive?

◆ ◆ ◆

The reason our political discourse has shifted so dramatically to the right over the past half century is because conservatives have a narrative advantage, one instigated by talk radio: the willingness to tell bad stories for political advantage.

Think about climate change. What's the story the left is stuck telling? That humans have been roaring drunk on fossil fuels for the past two centuries and are destroying the planet's thermostat, thanks to our unsustainable lust for convenience. The only way to rescue ourselves is to redesign our lives so as to reduce the rampant consumption that is the cornerstone of American culture and economic health. The conservative counter-narrative is that climate change is a hoax cooked up by scientists and tree-hugging elites who want to make you feel guilty for driving your SUV. Which story would you rather believe?

How about the financial meltdown of 2008? The left's version is that high rollers and predatory lenders, enabled by years of deregulation, turned mortgage debt into a massive profit source, exposing the corrosive greed at the heart of late-model capitalism. Wall Street CEOs made billions, while working- and middle-class Americans faced mass foreclosures and exploded pension plans. The right blamed the government for lending money to poor people.

The consensus view of the ensuing election was that Americans supported a sensible Democrat in reaction to eight years of Republican mismanagement. Talk radio portrayed Obama's election as a coup d'état that would result in terrorists being set free among us, a tax on personal carbon use, confiscation of guns, and the importation of sharia law.

I kind of wish I were exaggerating. I'm not. In talk radio, conservatives found an incubator for lurid conspiracies that would be laughed out of any editorial meeting. These theories didn't just reinvent the present, but the past. The New Deal and the Great Society programs weren't designed to help citizens avoid hardship but to consolidate the nefarious powers of the State.

The Tea Party's hysterical response to health-care reform wasn't a function of corporate PACs with chartered buses. It had been gestating for decades on the AM dial. Hosts had trained their listeners to regard any effort to strengthen the safety net as an assault on personal liberty. With the coming of Obamacare, "Statists would control not only the material wealth of the individual, but his physical well-being," host Mark Levin warned. A "politburo" would arise in which political appointees and bureaucrats decided "who lives and dies." Within months, this abstract notion had taken shape as "death panels" to euthanize the aged.

Republican politicians knew this claim was hot air but promoted it anyway. Mainstream media outlets debunked it endlessly. But as we know, false claims repeated often enough calcify into truths, especially among the elderly. As of last year, 60 percent of Americans still believed death panels were real, or weren't sure. Reporters devoted far more coverage to these false claims than the broadly popular measures actually contained within the Affordable Care Act.

This is what Nancy Pelosi meant when she told a room full of county officials, in 2010, "We have to pass the bill so that you can find out what is in it—away from the fog of the controversy." Talk radio hosts used the first half of this quote ("we have to pass the bill so that you can find out what is in it") to stoke outrage about the bill's allegedly secretive legislative genesis. Mainstream reporters then obediently threw this truncated quote back in Pelosi's face, completing the loop. Her effort to condemn the fog of controversy was quickly consumed by it.

◆ ◆ ◆

One of the reasons I've always been intrigued by the history of the Fairness Doctrine is because it embodies the war between two basics conceptions of American life: collectivism versus privatization.

Legislators imposed the Doctrine to insure that our discourse would take the form of a respectful exchange about issues of common concern. This is what Postman means when he talks about the quality of a culture being rooted in the Platonic idea of conversation. The repeal of the Doctrine reshaped American discourse into a series of arguments, mostly one-sided, and inevitably predicated on competing interests. That is, no longer a conversation at all.

Why did this happen? Because stories about competing interests proved far more seductive (and therefore profitable) than ones about shared goals. Successful talk radio hosts deftly pitted small businesses versus regulators, job creators versus unions, taxpayers versus bureaucrats, upstanding Christians versus catamites and abortionists. And so on.

The legislators and jurists who once spoke of the need to address "controversial issues" never envisioned a demagogue thundering for hours on end—nor a grid of howling pundits—as reasonable debate. In such media settings, the question is not: *How do we solve this problem?* It is: *Whose agenda will prevail?* Civic culture becomes a Hobbesian warzone.

To put it more broadly: capitalism *needed* a mechanism to shift popular attention away from the common good. Privatize ideology and you license all manner of privatization. Public lands become available for development and mining and drilling. Public schools give way to charters and vouchers. Public policy becomes a pig trough for special interests.

The current state of our prison industrial complex provides a rather transparent view of the process. The common good would be to reform criminal justice and reduce incarceration rates. But this conversation is drowned out by an argument about crime, one based on phony stats that pit law-abiding (read: white) citizens against dark-skinned assailants and immigrants. The private prison lobby contributes millions to help elect the law-and-order candidate. Among the first actions his administration takes is to rescind an order to phase out private prisons. Next, he enacts immigration policies that will fill private facilities with undocumented workers. A public crackdown becomes a private windfall.

◆ ◆ ◆

To focus on the financial endgame, though, is to overlook that old woman who trudged around Somerville with her homemade leaflets, heralding the prophecies of Michael Savage. She wasn't looking to pad corporate profits, after all. She was heeding a voice of divine revelation.

That sounds grandiose, but it's the reason conservative talk overtook AM radio: because there was a whole flock of Americans yearning for the spiritual comforts of dogma. What the most popular hosts were selling, ultimately, was the illusion of moral surety. They were never wrong, never at a loss for words, never confused or troubled or sorry. To maintain this pose required neutralizing any voices of opposition. This is what made the Fairness Doctrine such a bulwark against talk radio.

There are certainly other factors that explain its proliferation. Deregulation and media consolidation made syndication cheap and lucrative. Events such as the terrorist attacks of 2001, and Obama's election, spiked anxieties and ratings. But for conservative talk to thrive in the way it has required the forging of a new covenant, what amounts to an Unfairness Doctrine.

I mean by this that the Limbaughs and Savages of the world could only survive in a media landscape that allowed them to pose as journalists and experts without ever having to compete with actual journalists and experts, in which they could trumpet delusions and conspiracies without anyone to hold them accountable, in which they could craft a vision of America entirely insulated from the world of empirical fact or historical context. They had to be granted a safe space.

The glorious irony was that talk radio hosts used this safe space to insist that they were under siege, that the ideas they preached were, in fact, so disruptive to the status quo that elites would do anything to silence them. The promotion of this martyr complex was a rhetorical stratagem as old as the Bible ("Blessed are ye, when men shall revile you, and persecute you, and shall say all manner of evil against you falsely, for my sake.") Talk radio hosts didn't just inoculate their audience against criticism. They exhorted listeners to glory in condemnation. The establishment's rejection of their claims became proof of their validity.

Is any of this sounding familiar?

◆ ◆ ◆

To preserve their status as persecuted truth tellers, hosts had to create a suitable foil, the "liberal media" whose raison d'être was to spread disinformation to gullible Americans. Daniel Henninger, of the *Wall Street Journal*, put it like this: "Ronald Reagan tore down this wall [the Fairness Doctrine] in 1987 . . . and Rush Limbaugh was the first man to proclaim himself liberated from the East Germany of liberal media domination."

The link Henninger draws between the end of the Cold War and the rise of talk radio, though cheeky on his part, is no coincidence. For decades, conservative demagogues had vilified Russia and those who sympathized with the Communist cause. With the Evil Empire collapsing, Limbaugh and his comrades shifted their animus to a roster of domestic enemies. The goal was to convince listeners that *everyone* outside the reach of their voice harbored a corrupt agenda: politicians, media elites, academics, feminazis. Boil off the jocular bombast, and their skepticism aped totalitarian thought: dismiss any opponent as partisan, any inconvenient fact as left-wing propaganda.

But it's important to recognize that the essential function of talk radio was never to advocate for conservative positions. It was to build loyalty among listeners, so as to grow an audience for the sponsors. The most efficient way to do this was to get "dittoheads" to stop thinking for themselves, stop asking questions, stop exercising their critical faculty. The end was profit; the means was indoctrination.

◆ ◆ ◆

As entertainers, talk radio hosts succeed because they push limits. Some of this is Marketing 101. When you're hawking survivalist kits to senior citizens, you have to find a way to ratchet up the threat level. But talk radio hosts were the first media figures to grasp the implications of an unregulated marketplace, that journalistic integrity was irrelevant, even undesirable, in a pure attention economy.

Trump himself understood this intuitively, in part because he came of age as a tabloid celebrity in the New York City of the Seventies, where the most controversial voice on the airwaves was Bob Grant, a pioneer in the world of conservative talk radio.

Grant, who landed his gig on the liberal WMCA thanks to the Fairness Doctrine, blamed America's descent into "third worldism" on the Immigration and Nationality Act of 1965, and proposed a mandatory sterilization program to lower the birthrate among poor women. He was fired repeatedly for offensive remarks, only to be rehired. The more outrageous he became, the higher his ratings.

Grant's success underscored the quality Trump admired in his Manhattan mentor, Roy Cohn: shamelessness. To Cohn, the ultimate sin committed by his former boss, Joseph McCarthy, wasn't falsely accusing Americans of being Communists, or ruining thousands of lives. It was expressing shame. This is the precise moral outlook that talk radio has injected into the cultural bloodstream for the past 30 years.

"Anything down there about your souls?" Ishmael is asked by an acquaintance, after signing on with Ahab. "Oh, perhaps you hav'n't got any . . . No matter though, I know many chaps that hav'n't got any,—good luck to 'em; and they are all the better off for it. A soul's a sort of a fifth wheel to a wagon."

Trump didn't invent lying or hypocrisy or corruption. He simply imported the shameless self-promotion he flaunted in the worlds of real estate and entertainment to politics. In fact, he entered the arena with an advantage that virtually no one in the old guard media and political classes recognized: the GOP base hungered for a politician whose voice echoed the ones they tuned into daily. Talk radio had been transmuting despair into triumphant rage for decades. Trump merely inherited its audience share.

◆ ◆ ◆

In the past decade, the nexus of conservative media has migrated online, and lurched far enough to the right to openly embrace white nationalism and conspiracy theorists. One need look no further than Trump's prophet, Steve Bannon, the former editor of a website that specializes in both.

Trump got to know Bannon as a guest on his talk radio program, where the two conducted an open-air courtship. When Trump's campaign began to implode, he recruited Bannon to run the operation specifically because Bannon understood the power dynamics of the reactionary right's new media ecosystem—that a significant percentage of voters had been radicalized by talk radio and were therefore impervious to outside influences.

Bannon recognized that the Internet could be used to convert the conservative echo chamber into a bio weapons lab, where partisans viralize disinformation. That old woman with her homemade Michael Savage leaflets still existed. She still had time on her hands. Only now she had a computer and a Facebook page and Twitter. And she wasn't alone. She was part of a movement.

◆ ◆ ◆

It's impossible to say for certain what our political landscape would look like if the Fairness Doctrine hadn't been rescinded. Clearly, the advent of satellite radio and cable television would have complicated any regulation predicated on the scarcity of public airwaves.

It's much more apparent what the influence of conservative talk radio has been over the past 30 years. Those shocked by the rise of Trumpism simply weren't tuned to the right frequency. They had no idea that tens of millions of Americans had come to identify "leadership" with rambling narcissists and "courage" with outbursts that gave voice to their own inhibited bigotries. The targets Trump chose ("the media!," "the global elites!"), the crude branding ("Lyin Ted," "Crooked Hillary"), the catch phrases ("politically correct," "rigged system")—all of it derived from talk radio.

I don't listen to the genre much these days. I don't have to, really, because so much of its paranoid ideation has bled into the mainstream. The last time I tuned in was a month or so after the election. The first caller identified himself as a Teamster and life-long Democrat who bolted the party to back Trump. He now considered Democrats to be Communists, and was furious about the "paid protestors" showing up at town hall events to support Obamacare. If liberals continued on this path of violence, he vowed that he would be "the first one out on the street."

The next caller applauded the Teamster's courage. "The last guy you had on," he told the host, "he learned how to not to be a Democrat through talk radio. Not because of Obama. He started listening to you and you're his answer. And, you know, everybody gets a brain at a different time in life. I got mine when I was 25. So welcome aboard, buddy, and start talking it out, talking to people about talk radio, because that's what helped people get Donald Trump as president."

Trump is no more the engineer of this tectonic shift than he is a real estate magnate. He's the front man for a movement that took root and grew in direct correlation to the rise of talk radio. The GOP establishment embraced the medium because it helped shape hyper-partisan, misinformed voters who could be counted upon to embrace a politics of resentment over economic uplift. What they got in the bargain was a president who talks like Rush Limbaugh on the stump and thinks like a dittohead off it, a man who responds to accusations that he colluded with our chief foreign enemy by accusing his predecessor of spying on him. When asked to produce evidence, he can only point to the ranting of a talk radio host.

THE VAST RIGHT-WING CONSPIRACY
WAS JUST A CONSPIRACY

On the morning of October 29, 2016, I woke up and glanced at the front page of the *New York Times* and the small tender part of me that had held out hope for our free press—that it would begin to take the election seriously, would stop trafficking in bad stories before it was too late—died.

On that Saturday, ten days out from the election, there were plenty of stories worthy of coverage. A widening investigation, for instance, into how malfeasance among Republican state officials in Michigan led to the widespread poisoning of children in Flint, most of them poor African Americans. The nation's economic growth had surged to 2.9 percent, the highest rate in two years and hearty enough to prompt talk of a rate hike by the Federal Reserve. This is putting aside any of the dozens of policies proposed by the candidates vying for the presidency.

Instead, the front page carried three reports about a dormant investigation into Hillary Clinton's private email server. This was the only story covered above the fold, which made the matter appear as vital as, for instance, the declaration of war on another country, or a major terrorist attack—or the impeachment of a president.

Nine reporters contributed to these dispatches, which consumed two full pages inside. The "hook" of these stories was that FBI Director James Comey had found additional emails that might be related to his closed Clinton investigation. He didn't know because his agency hadn't reviewed them yet.

◆ ◆ ◆

To understand the significance of this front page to the course of American democracy requires some perspective.

It's important to recognize, right off the bat, that Hillary Clinton had been under investigation for more than three decades by the time she accepted her party's nomination. Americans mistrusted her not because of any criminal evidence against her, but because she'd been accused of wrongdoing for so long. This pattern had led to a predictable behavioral feedback loop. Clinton came off as guarded and defensive, which reinforced the idea that she had something to hide.

It would require another book to document all the reasons Clinton has been reviled. But one reason that is hardly ever cited is the fact that she was the first public figure to highlight the unholy alliances that radicalized conservatism.

"The great story here, for anybody willing to find it and write about it and explain it, is this vast right-wing conspiracy that has been conspiring against my husband since the day he announced for president," she noted, in an infamous 1998 interview on the *Today Show*. Her husband was embroiled in the Lewinsky scandal at the time, so most folks dismissed this statement as far-fetched.

I thought so too. But then something curious happened: I went to lunch with my girlfriend and her little sister, who was visiting from Iowa, where the two of them had grown up in a conservative family. At some point, the sister got to talking about the Clintons and mentioned, rather casually, that they had killed a lot of people. I laughed nervously but she assured me this was no joke. The Clintons had murdered dozens of their associates and, if I'm remembering correctly, also run a drug ring. Or maybe it was an underage sex ring. She had seen a documentary proving all this, which she urged me to see too.

This film does exist. *The Clinton Chronicles* was made in 1994, distributed by the couple's political opponents (including Reverend Jerry Falwell) and widely discussed on talk radio. A year after the film came out, a White House aide named Chris Lehane, working in relative obscurity, produced a 332-page memo called *The Communication Stream of Conspiracy Commerce.*

I have read this document. It is not far-fetched. On the contrary, it documents, in punishing detail, how unverified anti-Clinton conspiracies migrate from right-wing extremists to the Internet to conservative newspapers to GOP Congressmen, who mount inquiries, enabling the mainstream press to cover these allegations as legitimate stories. Lehane traced how specific stories traveled up the media food chain, providing dates and supporting exhibits. His blueprint exposed, two decades ago, the "close connection . . . between Republican elected officials and the right wing conspiracy industry," one that now looks like the beta version of what the Trump campaign, and Russian operatives, exploited to claim the 2016 election.

◆ ◆ ◆

A decade after Clinton attempted to expose these forces, she ran for president. A conservative group called Citizens United responded by producing another scathing documentary. The FCC ruled that the film was an "electioneering communication" and thus illegal to air under the Bipartisan Campaign Reform Act, which was designed to limit the influence of corporate money in politics. Citizens United sued and the Supreme Court ruled that corporations were entitled to the same First Amendment rights as people.

Once again, Hillary Clinton had gone to battle against conspiracy theorists bent on destroying her. The result was a legal ruling that handed her antagonists unlimited funding and allowed corporations and plutocrats to flood the American political system with propaganda.

One of the folks who quietly did this in 2016 was a reclusive hedge fund manager named Robert Mercer. Mercer is part of a growing faction of the super rich who no longer bother to make the case for supply-side economics. Instead, they insist that government coddles the poor and punishes the rich through taxation. This moral argument, which bluntly equates wealth with virtue, is essentially lifted from the pages of an Ayn Rand novel and repackaged as legislation by Paul Ryan. Mercer is "happy if people don't trust the government," one of his former colleagues told the investigative reporter Jane Mayer. "He wants it to *all* fall down."

Mercer spent much of the Nineties trying to convince co-workers that the Clintons were murderers and drug-runners, just like my ex-girlfriend's sister. The difference is that Mercer had a fortune to invest in shaping our democracy and, thanks to Citizens United, no limits on how to spend it.

So what did he do? He funded the work of a Machiavellian activist named Steve Bannon. He gave ten million dollars to Bannon's online conspiracy factory, Breitbart.com. He gave millions more to a firm called Cambridge Analytica, which uses, to quote Mayer, "secret psychological methods to pinpoint which messages are most persuasive to individual online viewers." The company has compiled detailed profiles on 220 million Americans.

The migration of anti-Clinton conspiracy theories from the fringes to the center of American political discourse was not some fluke. It was the inevitable result of a lengthy crusade, enabled by the erosion of campaign reform laws, funded by affluent zealots, and waged on Trump's behalf by professional and amateur cyber warriors.

Folks in the mainstream press couldn't understand why Trump routinely trotted out conspiracy theories. They either hadn't read, or didn't care to remember, Richard Hofstadter's warning that the paranoid style instills "heroic strivings for evidence to prove that the unbelievable is the only thing that can be believed." They didn't realize that a significant percentage of GOP primary voters *literally believed Clinton was a murderer.*

Trumpism essentially streamlined the conspiracy commerce process. The outlandish attacks he mounted thrilled his base and kept coverage from focusing on his policies, which were implausible and unpopular. The crowning irony was that all the "negative" coverage of Trump—engineered by the candidate himself—led the mainstream media outlets to compensate by ignoring Clinton's policy goals and focusing obsessively on . . . her email.

◆ ◆ ◆

So what *was* the story with Clinton's email?

As Secretary of State, Clinton was supposed to use a work phone with a work email. But she already had a personal phone with a personal email address and she didn't want to carry around two phones and use two email accounts. So she decided to use her personal phone and email—just as previous Secretaries of State such as Colin Powell had done. Her email account was housed on a private server Bill Clinton set up, which sounds kind of fishy until you consider that Clinton *was the former president of the United States.* He wasn't about to use a Yahoo server. He would have been hacked.

When Republicans discovered that Clinton had used her personal email address for work, they demanded the FBI investigate whether she had violated federal law regarding the handling of classified information. The FBI determined that some of Clinton's email traffic did contain classified information. But prosecutors needed to prove "malign intent" to convict. *Not wanting to carry two phones* didn't quite constitute that. So the FBI closed the case, declaring "no reasonable prosecutor" would charge Clinton.

To understand how this bureaucratic bungle became the defining narrative of the campaign, you have to realize that Clinton's character already had been cast into doubt. Virtually anything she did, from launching a philanthropic foundation to falling ill, was treated as a scandal. Because scandals are inherently speculative, because they can be nourished by an accretion of increasingly damning facts (i.e., Watergate) or a daisy chain of lurid conjecture and tangential inquisitions (i.e., Whitewater), they provide narrative longevity and focus within a news cycle that is otherwise frantic and scattershot.

By 2016, the media had become so habituated to retailing "Clinton scandals" that proof hardly mattered. It was as if Republican operatives had installed a smoke machine in Clinton headquarters, knowing the news trucks would rush out each time, eager to cover the fire.

Still, it is truly mind-boggling how disproportionately huge the coverage of Clinton's private email server story was. *Washington Post* political writer Chris Cillizza had written more than 50 items about Clinton's email by September, 2015, *more than a year before the election.* A full 11 percent of all campaign coverage across five major networks and six major papers focused on Clinton's email. The networks spent more time on Clinton email stories than all policy issues combined.

Please take a long moment to think about that.

◆ ◆ ◆

To take the email story seriously, as something truly nefarious and therefore worthy of more coverage than all policy issues combined, one would have to believe that Clinton consciously conspired to cover up explosive material, something so damning that it would rank as more heinous than, say, a candidate with shady business dealings across the globe refusing to release his tax returns. You would have to have reason to believe that her deleted emails contained evidence of, for instance, a covert effort to work with a foreign enemy. Did any of the thousands of editors and producers and reporters who pushed the Hillary email story believe this to be the case during the election?

No.

But they continued to cover it as a "political story" because it was virtually all the Republicans talked about. And it was all the Republicans talked about because it was the only "message" that united the establishment and Trump factions of the GOP, that brought the Wall Street Journal and Fox News into accord with talk radio and Bannon's online cabal. For journalists in search of a rationale more solid than the spectacle of a mob chanting *Lock Her Up*, former FBI Director James Comey provided the story's fig leaf of seriousness.

He made public statements about the Clinton email probe, in violation of agency protocol, not once but three times. In July, when he closed the investigation, he announced that her behavior had been "extremely careless." That same month, the FBI launched an investigation into Russian interference, and possible coordination with Trump campaign officials. Comey thought it was in the public interest to scold one candidate about her sloppy email protocol while remaining silent about the possibility that the other candidate might be actively engaged in acts of treason with America's chief foreign enemy.

It would be difficult to imagine a more obscene double standard.

In late October, Comey sent Congress a letter citing new emails that might be related to the closed Clinton probe. He didn't know—because his office had not looked at them. He did mention that the emails had been found on the computer of Anthony Weiner, the estranged husband of a Clinton aide and the disgraced congressmen best known for his X-rated texts.

Rather than behaving like the head of the FBI—issuing a subpoena and reviewing the emails in question for anything damning—he behaved like a tabloid editor, insinuating wrongdoing without a speck of evidence. He then issued a statement a few days before the election announcing that the subpoena had produced nothing, which kept email fever alive right up to Election Day.

◆ ◆ ◆

Let us return to that *New York Times* front page. The lead story ran under the banner NEW EMAILS FOUND IN WEINER INQUIRY JOLT 2016 ELECTION. It was one of those headlines that pretend the publication in question is merely "reporting" on an uproar when it is, in fact, authoring that uproar. What jolted the election wasn't Comey's letter, but the hysterical overreaction of media outlets such as the *Times*, which found occasion to mention "illicit text messages from Mr. Weiner to a 15-year-old girl in North Carolina" in its second paragraph. Translation: Hillary Clinton is mixed up with a pervert who preys on underage girls.

A second story focused on Comey's decision. The third piece—"With 11 Days to Go, Trump Says Revelation 'Changes Everything'"—might have been dictated from Trump Tower. The story functioned as an instruction manual for slow-witted NPR editors uncertain how to frame their segments. Here's how it began:

> Everything was looking up for Hillary Clinton. She was riding high in the polls, even seeing an improvement in trustworthiness. She was sitting on $153 million in cash. At 12:37 p.m. Friday, her aides announced that she planned to campaign in Arizona, a state that a Democratic presidential candidate has carried only once since 1948.
>
> Twenty minutes later, October delivered its latest big surprise.

In case anyone missed the SUBTLE SUBTEXT, the authors were promising that the race was close again. Trump "exulted in his good fortune" and promised to "batter Mrs. Clinton as a criminal in the race's final week and a half" while the revelation "set off a frantic and alarmed scramble inside Mrs. Clinton's campaign . . ."

To reiterate: the true source of Trump's "good fortune," and Clinton's panic, wasn't Comey's letter. It was the predictable and utterly cynical repackaging of an investigative fishing expedition into a game changing event. "I think it's the biggest story since Watergate," Trump crowed of Comey's letter. The bad stories peddled by the *Times* created this very impression. And this impression created a new reality.

◆ ◆ ◆

Reporters and editors have been quick to dismiss the idea that the email story ushered a dangerously unqualified demagogue into the Oval Office. No, it must have been something more substantial, more serious: working class economic frustrations or demographic anxieties or Clinton's foolish decision to ignore those rust belt swing states.

But the data on this was, to quote Nate Silver, "pretty straightforward." The Comey letter was the lead story for six of the seven days leading up to the election, during which Clinton lost three percentage points in the polls. The race was decided by a tiny fraction of voters in swing states leery of both candidates. These voters broke for Trump in the final two weeks of the campaign and did so largely because they kept hearing about Clinton's emails.

Take Pennsylvania, where the majority of voters approved of Obama and thought Trump was dishonest, erratic, and unqualified. Why didn't Clinton win there? According to Dan Hopkins, a researcher at the University of Pennsylvania, the key was the email story, which pushed marginal voters into the Trump camp.

And here's another nauseating irony that journalists should be force-fed: the nebulous nature of the email story, the fact that reporters couldn't explain what Clinton had done wrong and why it mattered—in other words, the very factors that *should have disqualified it as a story*—actually magnified its impact.

Why? Because voters viewed any report involving "Clinton" and "email" as part of same miasma. All those Russians operatives who hacked into DNC email accounts, the ones dispatched by the Kremlin to smear Clinton? They became another reason to doubt her.

♦ ♦ ♦

Was the editorial sensibility that led editors at the *Times* to assign those three Comey stories, then splash them across the front page 10 days before an election, the same one that guided the *Times* during the Watergate era? Was it a sensibility that sought to divine the moral importance of proposed stories— or their perceived ability to capture and market sensation?

Times editors could have treated Comey's letter like the nothing burger they knew it to be, after all, just as they could have decided that the Russian campaign to subvert our election mattered more than the stolen data. Those decisions would have sent an unmistakable message to readers and the rest of the media. Instead, they bowed to various pressures: the desire to goose the election narrative, to appear even-handed, to remain relevant in a media landscape overrun by tabloid norms.

Over the past year, journalists at the *Times* and elsewhere, have sought penance by working frantically to expose Trump's corruption and incompetence. We now know that his campaign attempted to collude with Russia, that multiple staffers met with Russians, that the FBI obtained a federal warrant to surveil a Trump advisor on the suspicion that he was a Kremlin spy. We know Trump was involved in a real estate deal that appears to have helped fund an Iranian group that sponsors terrorism, and that a senior advisor is a member of an organization with Nazi sympathies. It goes on and on.

But here's the point: all of these stories existed *during* the campaign. And it was incumbent upon the media to expose them back then, so Americans had a full accounting of the

Republican candidate. That's what the media is supposed to do in elections: vet the candidates.

This is especially important when one of the candidates has no public record as an elected official and a mountain of lawsuits and bankruptcies and a campaign manager with deep ties to the Kremlin and another whose website stokes white nationalism, and a shadowy set of financial entanglements, none of which he will make public by releasing his tax returns.

That's not a red flag for the media. It's a red sea.

When newspapers such as the *New York Times* assign nine reporters to cover a fake scandal, those folks are not focused on telling other, more consequential stories. The resources eaten up by their stories aren't devoted to vetting.

My point here isn't to lionize Clinton. Months before her nomination—back when I was lobbying my wife to support Bernie Sanders—I wrote about her flaws as a candidate, her buck raking speeches to Wall Street firms, her support for the Iraq War, and so on. My overriding concern, though, was that the media would continue to typecast her as crooked rather than examining her policies or qualifications.

♦ ♦ ♦

In moments of errant rage during the campaign, I found myself conducting little thought experiments. How would the media react if tape emerged of Hillary Clinton bragging to one of her female aides? *Hey, you know what I like to do when I see one of those hot little consular attaches? I'll just walk up to him and grab him by the cock. Just like that. Maybe juggle his balls, stick a thumb up his ass. They let you do anything when you're Secretary of State.*

Then I ticked down the list.

What if Hillary Clinton mocked a disabled journalist from Fox News? What if she introduced herself as a candidate by inveighing against hillbilly rapists? What if she urged her supporters to beat up protestors at her rallies? What if she called John McCain a loser for being captured? What if she had been sued by the federal government for racial discrimination? What if she was under investigation for defrauding students at her fake university? What if she used charitable donations to her foundation to purchase self-portraits to hang in her resorts? Or made political contributions to prosecutors investigating her? What if she refused to cough up her tax returns?

If we can agree that any of these actions would have spelled the end of her campaign, what does it mean that our culture created a safe space for her opponent to behave in these ways *while running for president*? And by safe space, I don't just mean within his party, or partisan outlets.

I mean that the media, as an institution, provided Trump a soft filter and a foil. The cable shows faithfully presented him in front of adoring crowds. Pundits chewed over his words and eschewed his policies. Producers stocked their panels with shrieking surrogates who reduced any war of ideas into a binary brawl. It was this quality of calculated rancor that Trump exploited time and again. If he lied, he was lying to the media and it was what they deserved, because they were liars.

Consider what happened every time Trump had to go before the American people during the debates—unmediated, that is. Most viewers recognized, almost at once, that he was unfit for office.

◆ ◆ ◆

By contrast, consider the perspective offered by the Showtime series *The Circus*, a documentary style look at the election, hosted by veteran political reporters Mark Halperin and John Heilemann. The show introduced candidate Trump at a packed arena in Florida. "Every country in the world is ripping us off! It's a really bad scene, and it's going to continue if you put any of these other people." Later, Trump did a little minority outreach ("I love Mexican people, I have thousands of Hispanics who work for me") before a rousing finale: "The American dream is dead, but we're going to make it bigger and better and stronger than ever before." As the screen filled with slow-mo footage of the candidate winking and pointing, Heilemann declared that Trump "played the crowd like a maestro. Rock star quality. You can't buy it. You can't bottle it. You either have it or you don't."

Right.

It may seem gratuitous to criticize a show like *The Circus*. But panting infomercials of this sort—served up by Beltway pros—reveal how degraded our journalistic standards have become. These guys make no effort to vet Trump, to investigate his financial history, to outline his policies, or to critique his worldview. They judge him purely as an entertainer. Politics has always involved showmanship. But this is precisely why reporters exist: to puncture the spectacle of political theater.

As I listened to Heilemann's nauseating voice-over, I kept recalling the take Hunter S. Thompson offered back in 1972:

> The whole framework of the presidency is getting out of hand. It's come to the point where you almost can't run unless you can cause people to salivate and whip on each other with big sticks. You almost have to be a rock star to get the kind of fever you need to survive in American politics . . . The main problem in any democracy is that crowd-pleasers are generally brainless swine who can go out on a stage & whup their supporters into an orgiastic frenzy—then go back to the office & sell every one of the poor bastards down the tube for a nickel apiece.

Thompson didn't pretend to be some "objective" witness to the 1972 election. He sized up Nixon and judged him to be paranoid, deceptive, and corrupt. But more broadly, he was distressed by a political system that would nominate a man of such low character. His willingness to say so made him an outlier, a gonzo renegade. But a proper reading of history is that Thompson was the only sane actor in that particular election. He voiced dissent while the rest of the press was busy manufacturing consent. "Jesus! Where will it end?" he wrote, two years before Watergate broke. "How low do you have to stoop in this country to be president?"

At what point did the folks in charge of our major media outlets ask themselves this question? At what point did they know that Trump had stooped too low? They knew all along. But so long as our free press operates as a for-profit enterprise, its managers are duty-bound to sell whatever we're willing to buy.

Media outlets presented the race as a rank spectacle because we couldn't resist the urge to hate watch. There was something pornographic in the arrangement, a familiar tension between grotesque fascination and shame. On election night, when it finally dawned on the anchors and viewers that Trump had won the Electoral College, you could sense the shock of a mass delusion being shattered in real time. That delusion amounted to a coup we had engineered against ourselves, arising from unseriousness and bad stories.

GIVE US YOUR TIRED, YOUR POOR,
YOUR HUDDLED MASSES

The man I came to know as Shane O'Neill was born in a tiny Yugoslavian village. When he was eight years old, he found an encyclopedia with several black-and-white photos of the American West and decided that he would become a cowboy. At 15, he left home to work as a dishwasher on a cruise ship and when the ship made port in Chicago he snuck into America with only 200 dollars and an English/Serbo-Croatian dictionary to his name.

By the time I met him, 15 years later, he wore tooled leather chaps, silver spurs, a holster housing an antique Colt .45, and a horseshoe mustache bigger than an actual horseshoe. Shane had just become a legal citizen of the United States, though he looked more like a figure from an Old West daguerreotype. I wanted to learn more about his life, so I went to visit him at a ranch in the foothills of the Guadalupe

Mountains in southern New Mexico, where he worked as an itinerant cowboy.

The more I learned about Shane, the more unlikely his story became. He had taken his American name from a kindly rancher who looked after him when he first arrived in America. He spoke seven languages. He made his own clothing. He had a wife and a two-year-old son and he lived in a battered trailer and worked 14-hour days and was paid $850 per month, a salary he set himself. He appeared impervious to fear or pain.

On the first day of my visit, I watched him goad a brown bull into a truck by yanking its tail. The animal delivered a swift kick to his midriff, a blow Shane refused to acknowledge until later that night, when he stripped off his shirt and I saw the red, hoof-shaped welt on his stomach.

Shane occupied a curious place within the cultural milieu of ranch hands. He worked as the de facto supervisor of the Mexican *vaqueros*, from whom he had learned the trade. He spoke Spanish almost exclusively, worked and ate with his crew and told me, repeatedly, that vaqueros were "the only true cowboys," the ones who knew how to read the land, to round up stray cattle, mend fences, check wells. In other words, Shane was kind of an elitist. He continually mocked "gringo cowboys" for having no heart, for sticking close to the ranch, cruising around in their trucks and operating the modern equipment. Shane had one other big thing in common with the vaqueros: he had spent years living in fear of being deported, trying to stay one step ahead of the immigration authorities.

But here's where things got really odd, because Shane's view of immigrants was quite harsh. "Nobody wants to work hard here, especially people from foreign countries," he grumbled. "They come to America and want an easy job in the big city. They think of America only as money, as an escape from the hard life."

To Shane, cities were corrupt and frightening places, where evil festered and the pace of life had gone haywire. He had a recurring dream in which all the trucks in America ran out of gas and he would be asked to lead a cattle drive to Dodge City, Kansas. "I want to live slow," he told me, toward the end of our time together, "with the land, like an Indian."

◆ ◆ ◆

I thought a lot about Shane during the election because he seemed to embody so many of the conflicting stories we tell about our history and ourselves. He was a fiercely patriotic immigrant who had risked everything to reach the United States, where he had fashioned himself into a cowboy who dreamed of living like an Indian. His vision of citizenship was bled through with a dark nostalgia, a longing to make America great again by returning to a bygone era, fortifying the borders, walling off the cities, magically reversing the morally corrosive march of modernity.

As enlightened as he often sounded, his thinking was polarized: there were good and bad immigrants, good and bad parts of America. Once you started to think this way, you became susceptible to a politics based not on principles but tribal identity. Inevitably, this led to candidates who wooed whites in rural and semi-rural areas by demonizing immigrants. And at that point, a guy like Shane—without even meaning to—was in accord with a nationalist movement that would not only criminalize the *vaqueros* he revered, but result in his own deportation.

◆ ◆ ◆

Americans have been working through this paradox since well before our founding. We're a nation of immigrants and immigrant bashers.

One of George Washington's first decrees as president was to encourage immigration. He recognized that the new Republic would be made great by welcoming "not only the Opulent and respectable Stranger, but the oppressed and persecuted of all Nations And Religions." The rigors of the process acted as a quality control filter, insuring that new Americans were precisely the sort of intrepid, ambitious people who would fuel our national expansion.

They were also conveniently desperate, and thus routinely exploited for cheap labor, crowded into ghettos and tenements, and reviled for political purposes. You can trace this legacy of hazing from the ranks of Chinese who perished building our railways to the Irish targeted by the anti-immigrant, anti-Catholic fervor of the Know Nothings to the quintet of Italians lynched at the turn of the 19th century, about whom the *New York Times* had this to say: "These sneaking and cowardly Sicilians, the descendants of bandits and assassins, who have transported to this country the lawless passions, the cut-throat practices, and the oath-bound societies of their native country, are a pest to us without mitigation. Our own rattle-snakes are as good citizens as they . . . Lynch law was the only course open to the people of New Orleans to stay the issue of a new license to the Mafia to continue its bloody practices."

The nativist impulse—often obscured by the degradations of slavery, Jim Crow, and segregation—has persisted as a powerful undercurrent amid otherwise advancing tides of American tolerance. And it has gained force in the past few decades, as politicians and corporations have sought to shift the blame for our ruthless domestic inequalities onto foreign targets: globalization and immigrants.

It was no mistake that Trump launched his candidacy with attacks on Mexican and Muslim immigrants; they had become the designated scapegoats of GOP primary voters. It didn't matter that these populations posed almost no risk to the good people of Des Moines, nor that deportations had spiked under Obama while terrorist attacks plunged. Because the rhetoric wasn't really about providing economic support or homeland security. It was about converting white self-hatred into electoral empowerment.

Consider the label Trump invoked to describe his base: "the forgotten man." The term has a long and revealing history in our discourse. It was coined in 1883 by the social scientist William Graham Sumner, who advanced an argument that has become the cornerstone of modern conservatism: that industrious Americans are continually being victimized by the undeserving poor.

Franklin Delano Roosevelt appropriated the name to describe those at the bottom of the economic pyramid, and most in need of a New Deal. Richard Nixon swiped the term back, using it to woo blue-collar workers to a party historically aligned with the business class. His pitch took on an overt racial cast. The Forgotten Man was white. Those mooching off him—whether Welfare Queen or undocumented worker—were brown.

The population in question here is the same one Hannah Arendt referred to as "superfluous," and that Richard Rorty predicted would seek out a strongman: whites unable to compete in a global economy against those willing to work longer hours for less pay. Just as the story of race granted disenfranchised Caucasians "the psychological wage of whiteness," nationalism granted them "the psychological wage of Americanness," the belief that citizenship imbued them with an inherent moral superiority to foreigners, a set of rights and virtues forever under siege.

◆ ◆ ◆

It took me a week of living on the border with Mexico to see what a crock this was. I could see, almost at once, that Mexicans worked harder than Americans, in particular those who snuck into the United States.

I've mentioned the small armada of day maids who waded across the Rio Grande at dawn. Just as striking were the *colonias* of Juarez, shanty towns built by migrants from the interior who had come for jobs in the *maquiladoras*, so-called "twin plants" in which the American plant was a tiny executive outpost, while its Mexican counterpart housed hundreds of workers who assembled circuit boards or sorted coupons for a few dollars a day.

I watched entire neighborhoods take shape in a matter of weeks. Migrants staked claims and erected homes from scrap metal and wood and old tires. They carved out roads and pirated electricity and collected water in rain barrels. It was impossible to gaze upon such scenes, a few hundred feet away, and not draw comparisons to the American way of life: shiny cars rolling down immaculate highways, our lavish, climate-controlled homes and apartments, our casual use of adjectives such as "starving" to describe the experience of having to wait a few extra minutes at the drive-thru.

And I remember, too, the day a woman named Lupe showed up outside my apartment with her daughter. She was a friend of my girlfriend, in need of food and clothing for her five children, one of whom, a little girl of perhaps seven, stood behind her. All at once, as we were talking there on the sidewalk, a blob of white liquid landed on Lupe's head. Neither of us could understand what had happened. Then we looked up and saw pair of fat pigeons perched above us on the phone wires. We stood there in excruciating silence. The little girl said nothing. Her eyes were dark and unsurprised.

There was nowhere to print a story like this, even though it said more about living on the border than anything else I ever wrote. To live in El Paso was to ignore, every day, even when one of them was standing right in front of you with her young daughter, a vast set of people getting shat upon by fate.

◆   ◆   ◆

I'm not suggesting that Mexicans are all noble martyrs and gringos are all spoiled brats. I'm suggesting that the rage Americans direct at immigrants has almost nothing to do with how they impact our lives. The anger arises from a psychological need within certain Americans to view their citizenship as a sacred affirmation of their own cunning and grit rather than dumb luck.

American politicians, particularly conservatives, have long stoked this delusion, preaching a doctrine of personal responsibility that cleverly flatters the most vulnerable of their constituents by painting them as victims of a government determined to rob them of liberty, rather than what they often are: humiliated recipients of public services and entitlements.

In a mature democracy, these folks would investigate the sources of their strife and rise up against (for instance) corporations that ship jobs overseas, a billionaire donor class that buys elections, and politicians who obediently reward CEOs and punish workers. In America, forgotten men and women rage instead against their own dependence.

Trump was merely the logical endpoint of this scam, a casino capitalist with gold toilets who passed himself off as a populist by pledging to raze Washington. He ditched supply side economics for the slang of the get-rich seminars to which he leased his name. *Health care for everyone! Zero unemployment! You'll win so much you'll get sick of winning!* Trump needed voters to view themselves as the patrons in the great gambling house of democracy, and a remarkable number couched their support in these terms. They were ready to "take a chance" on him, to "roll the dice," to revel in the stage show and the free drinks and the sparkling promise that one daring bet would beat the house.

In this sense, hatred of immigrants was essential to the pitch. Because immigrants represented the traditional path to prosperity: years of hard work, the slow accretion of opportunity, a durable faith in the American dream. All of this was anathema to Trumpism, which could offer only the short cut of the Ponzi scheme.

The pledge Trump made was one of racial and national patronage. White natives would feel like winners again—not because they won anything but because brown interlopers would be made to lose. Shane O'Neil could have his fantastical cattle drive to Dodge City, but the vaqueros who taught him how to ride the range would wind up in a jail cell.

BAD STORY #16

THE COLD WAR IS OVER
(AND WE WON!)

M ost of what we call "history" amounts to an accounting of how great empires rise and fall. It's a different
story each time, but there is one common thread. Over and
over, empires are marred by internal divisions, which make
them vulnerable to a foreign threat. The Persians were ripe
for conquest long before Alexander the Great arrived. Ditto
the Mongols and the Romans and the Aztecs, who were sub-
dued by a handful of Spanish Conquistadors in alliance with
Montezuma's enemies.

This is also, to some mysterious degree, what just happened in America. We don't yet know the full extent of the
Russian effort to influence the 2016 election, and we may never get the entire story. But we do know that our chief global
rival deployed an army of hackers and operatives and bots to
help elect Donald Trump. We know that the Russians were
working to help Trump claim the GOP nomination and gen-

eral election. We know that a galling number of the candidate's team—from volunteers and advisors to core staff and family—eagerly solicited help from Russians promising dirt on Clinton, even meeting with them in Trump Tower. (By any rational definition, this is attempted collusion). We know Russian hacking resulted in thousands of damning stories about Clinton, and that cyber warriors—aided by Trump partisans and other disgruntled actors—viralized more outlandish smears against her.

We also know that the Russians were wildly successful. By the time Election Day rolled around, the fake news items they planted and promoted had become the most popular on the Internet. Vladimir Putin's handpicked candidate lost the popular vote by three million and won the presidency.

◆ ◆ ◆

One of the conditions that has always limited the American imagination is the unique nature of our history and geography. We're bordered by two oceans and a pair of weak nations. We've never been invaded by a foreign enemy. We control and consume a huge percentage of the planet's resources, and possess the most powerful military on Earth.

During the height of the Cold War, Americans worried about a nuclear attack. And more recently, we've become perpetually jittery about terrorism. But it has always been hard for us to envision our country infiltrated by another. Our anxieties about foreign influence tend to take the form of domestic witch-hunts. Again: it is our national habit to take our grievances seriously, but not our vulnerabilities.

A British intelligence agency first detected suspicious "interactions" between Russian agents and Trump associates as early as 2015. Agents from four other countries—Germany, Australia, Poland, and Estonia—detected the same patterns over the next few months, and tipped off their American counterparts. But the FBI didn't launch a formal investigation of the matter until late July of 2016. U.S. agencies "were asleep," is how one source put it.

When Estonian intelligence officials have to light a fire under the FBI to get them to investigate potentially treasonous conduct by an American presidential campaign, it is fair to say that the folks charged with protecting us from foreign infiltration have grown complacent.

But it wasn't just our spies who blew this off. Our political leadership said almost nothing about the Russian intrusion. Our Fourth Estate served as publicity agents for Putin. And most voters shrugged. It was as if the scariest moments of the Cold War—the Cuban Missile Crisis, the downing of Korean Air Lines Flight 007 and the Able Archer 83 exercise that followed—had been erased from the public's memory. And in a sense, that *is* what happened.

Because for most Americans the Cold War ended on November 9, 1989, the day the Berlin Wall was toppled. We had won in a rout, as President Reagan promised, and reduced the Evil Empire to a Baltic backwater ruled by alcoholics and oligarchs. This left America as the planet's sole superpower, a proud capitalist fortress impervious to the meddling of some vanquished rival. That's the story we've told ourselves for 25 years.

◆ ◆ ◆

But try to imagine how an ambitious young KGB officer living in the Dresden of 1989 is viewing the same events, a man born in the age of Sputnik and so keen to emulate the spies portrayed in Soviet cinema that he takes up martial arts and foreign languages as a teenager.

Imagine how he feels as he burns the agency's files to keep them from falling into the hands of pro-democracy demonstrators. Imagine how he feels in 1991, as the Soviet Union officially dissolves and George H.W. Bush tells to the world, "The biggest thing that has happened in the world in my life, in our lives, is this: By the grace of God, America won the Cold War."

Now imagine that same former KGB officer shrewdly ascending to the leadership of Russia, eliminating opponents, silencing journalists, consolidating power. Imagine that the driving force in his life is to restore the stature of his disgraced homeland, to Make Russia Great Again, as it were. Jump into that guy's head and ask yourself: Is the Cold War really over?

◆ ◆ ◆

Now ask yourself what you would do if you were Vladimir Putin and word arrived at the Kremlin, in June of 2015, that Donald Trump is actually running for president of the United States. Trump is no stranger to Putin. He's a familiar figure in post-Soviet Russia, not just as a TV celebrity who throws beauty contests, but as a real estate impresario hungry to profit off his brand, and not especially discerning when it comes to his partners.

Like many global businessmen, Trump runs his finances through a web of front companies and offshore accounts, and takes a famously lax approach to vetting foreign partners. Because Trump refuses to release his tax returns, nobody really knows how much money he owes and to whom. But Putin surely knows all about Trump's business ties to oligarchs and organized crime figures in Russia and Ukraine. Which means the Russian autocrat is in the odd but enviable position of knowing more about the finances of an American presidential aspirant than the voters who will potentially elect him. He may even have enough damning information to blackmail Trump. Only he knows for sure.

But there are plenty of other reasons Trump represents a dream candidate. To begin with, Putin has invaded Ukraine and intervened in Syria. Obama responded to the Ukrainian incursion with sanctions, and Hillary Clinton has promised an even more aggressive approach. Putin knows that any further Russian expansionism can only flourish if the U.S. changes course dramatically and retreats from the world stage. The Trump agenda—such as it is—calls for America to do just that, to stop playing global policeman, to cut funding to NATO, and to focus instead on securing American borders and scotching trade deals.

On the stump, Trump paints America's government as hopelessly corrupt. His specific plans, however, are not designed to foster reform. They are ruses of the sort employed by leaders from less developed countries: building a border wall, banning religious minorities, attacking the courts and the press.

Putin knows he can't defeat the United States on the battlefield, or in the global marketplace. The effort to keep pace in these arenas triggered the demise of the Soviet experiment. But Trump represents an unprecedented opportunity. He knows almost nothing about history or governance and celebrates this ignorance. He has no conception of American interests abroad, apart from his personal interests, because he sees the world as purely transactional. He is, in this sense, the logical culmination of late-model capitalism, a human corporation driven by financial gain and personal glory, willing to say or do anything to win.

His temperament suggests that he will pursue no coherent agenda beyond winning the next news cycle. His domestic policies, to the extent they succeed, will widen the cultural, economic, and political divides he exploited on the campaign trail and intensify the cynicism with which most Americans regard government. And he will respond to foreign provocations guided not by expertise and caution but the reckless bidding of injured pride. In short, Trump will destabilize the United States and reduce its standing in the world.

Now just imagine, for a little longer, that you are Vladimir Putin and you are watching Donald Trump's candidacy catch fire, undimmed, in some ways fueled, by his taunts and deceptions, the buzz of round-the-clock coverage, the roaring crowds and soaring poll numbers. These must look to you like the seeds of a reckoning, the bill coming due on America's long descent into decadence and distraction, proof that any society ruled by the vulgar incentives of profit is destined to select a vulgar profiteer as its leader.

It's probably too much to hope for, but some part of you must recognize the stakes here. This is not just another foreign election. Trump is a kind of geopolitical unicorn, the useful idiot abruptly elevated into a Manchurian candidate. Sure, it's a long shot, but if you're Putin you can see the payout: the chance to elect a man capable of initiating what the Soviet Union never could—an era of permanent American decline.

◆ ◆ ◆

Am I suggesting that Putin dreams of reinstating Communist world domination? No. He knows that Russia will have to forge a new path in a globalized world, something more like a corporatist oligarchy. But he also recognizes that the Cold War was never a battle for military or economic supremacy. It's a war of ideas being fought, ultimately, by political means.

This is why Putin began encouraging his military leaders years ago to concentrate on developing cyber warfare. And the reason he began to fund think tanks. One of them, the Russian Institute for Strategic Studies, drew up a specific plan to influence the 2016 race, which was circulated at the highest levels of the Kremlin. As a former senior U.S. intelligence official told Reuters, "Putin had the objective in mind all along, and he asked the institute to draw him a road map."

Putin understood that Trumpism caught fire because our ballyhooed democratic institutions—fair elections, a free press, political compromise—no longer obtained. What he saw instead was a population largely insulated from danger and therefore largely indifferent to its political fate, easily disenchanted if not openly enraged, paranoid, credulous, screen-addicted, and in the thrall of media companies driven either by profit or ideology. He saw a nation ripe for subversion.

◆ ◆ ◆

This subversion began with Russian hackers breaking into the DNC, like the Watergate burglars of yore. But how could Putin, as the leader of a hostile foreign power, fence his stolen goods to the American public?

In June, he tried the direct route, releasing a trove of emails through a newly created website. Alas, the material was difficult to search and bore notes in Russian. The result was a *Washington Post* story that focused not on the data but its source.

So what did Putin do next? Like any shrewd cartel boss, he laundered his contraband using a front company: Wikileaks. According to a dossier prepared by the former British intelligence agent Christopher Steele, the Russians did this with full knowledge of Trump campaign officials. Wikileaks provided all parties "plausible deniability." The dossier also alleged that Russians had been working to promote Trump's candidacy for years, and that they had gathered enough damning material on his financial and sexual dealings to blackmail him.

Whether or not you believe the contents of this dossier, the middlemen at Wikileaks served a second crucial function. They made the data easily searchable, and timed releases for maximum sales.

On the eve of the Democratic National Convention, Wikileaks published 19,000 hacked emails, a handful of which revealed tensions between the Clinton and Sanders campaigns, and the DNC. Reporters—the street-level corner boys in my tortured analogy—snapped up this junk and shot it straight into the American political bloodstream. A *Post* headline neatly summed up the media frenzy: "Here Are the Latest, Most Damaging Things in the DNC Emails." Trump responded to the leak by entreating Russian hackers to find Clinton's "missing" emails, a jovial act of treason that effectively linked the two separate scandals.

On October 7, Wikileaks released thousands more emails, including drafts of Clinton's paid speeches to Wall Street firms. This dump came one hour after a video surfaced in which Trump bragged of grabbing women by their pussies.

There was never any doubt that conservative outlets and Trump officials would hype this material. What's remarkable is that the rest of the media went right along, without ever asking themselves: *Are we being used here? And if so, to what end?*

◆ ◆ ◆

We also know that Trump surrounded himself with guys such as Paul Manafort and Michael Flynn, who had long and shady histories with Russia. (As this book went to press, Manafort had been indicted and Flynn had plead guilty to lying to the FBI.) The relationship between Trump policy advisor Carter Page and Russian operatives was so cozy that the FBI actually sought a secret court order to monitor his communications last summer. This required them to convince a Foreign Intelligence Surveillance Court judge that there was probable cause to believe Page was acting as an agent of a foreign power, (i.e., as a Russian spy). Trump jettisoned all three men after the press began to write about their relationships with Russia. But every day brings new revelations of undisclosed meetings and financial ties between Trumpworld and Putinworld.

For most of the campaign, Trump did not appear to understand how sinister all this might seem. According to one former advisor, the candidate successfully lobbied GOP officials to soften their stance toward Russia in the party platform. He frequently praised Putin, claiming he was a stronger leader than Obama, and expressed delight with the Russian hackers (and the Wikileakers) assailing Clinton.

Whatever the full extent of the collusion with Russia was, the more disturbing question is why the interests of the Trump campaign and the Kremlin aligned in the first place. The degree to which they acted in concert is uncanny. In

October, for instance, as polls showed Trump trailing by a wide margin, the same Kremlin think tank that drew up the roadmap for Russian interference circulated a paper arguing that operatives should promote claims about voter fraud, to cast doubt on the legitimacy of the election results. Within days, Trump himself began to raise the same questions.

Over the past year, the nature and scope of Putin's campaign has become more discernible. His ultimate goal, beyond bashing Clinton, was to divide Americans by exploiting cultural resentments, often the same ones Trump stokes for political gain. When our president fumes about NFL player protests or Confederate monuments or gun rights, he isn't just "shoring up his base." He's doing Putin's bidding.

◆ ◆ ◆

I think here of the moment, aboard the Pequod, when Tashtego first sights a pod of sperm whales and a private retinue, enlisted by Ahab and till now hidden from view, melts into view, "five dusky phantoms that seemed fresh formed out of air." The crew is stunned by this subterfuge, and confused as to the precise motive of Ahab's enigmatic harpooner, a Parsee named Fedallah. They speculate that he is the devil in disguise. Some believe he intends to kidnap Ahab.

"The men looked dubious at him," Ishmael tells us, "half uncertain . . . whether indeed he were a mortal substance, or else a tremulous shadow cast upon the deck by some unseen being's body."

Was this was not the role Putin played in our election?

◆ ◆ ◆

Putin knew America was too powerful to attack with bombs or sanctions, so he attacked us with bad stories. Most of his dirty work was carried out by American reporters and pundits and demagogues and Internet trolls who eagerly trafficked anti-Clinton hacks and slanders.

As a former KGB officer, Putin surely recognized our conservative media complex for what it was: an increasingly influential propaganda machine. He knew a significant minority of our population no longer cleaved to traditional standards of journalistic verification, and openly embraced conspiracies. He knew that barely half of all registered voters bothered to show up at the polls, which magnified the power of such partisans. He knew our corporate media had become increasingly driven by a tabloid mentality, which led them to promote Trump to the detriment of his rivals and to the exclusion of policy.

What Putin probably could not have foreseen was the astonishing complicity of our law enforcement officials and political leaders.

FBI Director Comey, as we have seen, cast public asper-
sions on Clinton while remaining silent about his agency's
investigation of the Trump team, which included a *suspected
Russian spy*. As it turns out, Comey asked President Obama
months before the election if he could write an Op-Ed about
Russian interference. This piece wouldn't have mentioned the
Trump/Russia investigation, but it would have alerted Americans to the threat, which Comey believed included an effort
by Russian hackers to break into voter registration systems.

Obama said no. He was afraid Republicans would accuse
him of trying to sway the election for Clinton. He also was
concerned that raising doubts about the legitimacy of the
election would reinforce the narrative that the Kremlin and
Trump were pushing.

Think about how crazy that is. Trump spent the last two
weeks of the campaign insisting, without evidence, that the
election was rigged against him. At the same time, the president of the United States—provided with extensive evidence
of Russian interference in our election, and the possibility of
treasonous collusion by the Republican campaign—chose
not to say anything because he believed telling the American
people the truth would do more harm than good to our democratic process.

Congressional leaders who received briefings on Russian
interference also stayed mum. The one exception was the
Senate's top Democrat Harry Reid, who implored Comey to

go public with his "explosive" investigation into the Trump/ Russia connection. Had Obama joined Reid in this call, had the media taken these claims seriously, had pressure been applied to Comey, he might have started worrying about the secrets he was keeping on Trump's behalf.

◆ ◆ ◆

So if you're Putin watching all this play out, what conclusion are you left to draw? It must be this: that America's realpolitik has become so warped, so riven with internal divisions, so ethically enfeebled, that the sitting president can't even speak to his own people about the Kremlin's efforts to subvert their election. He must see that U.S. political and media systems now operate largely in reaction to the prosecutorial hysteria of a conservative minority that imposes its will through intimidation, seductive misinformation, a blind tribal unity. How different can this "democracy" look from his own government?

Think about what Putin already has seen. The election of 2000, in which another conservative candidate lost the popular vote and was on the brink of losing the electoral recount—in the state governed by his own brother—until his allies on the Supreme Court intervened to award him the presidency.

As for the men Trump appoints to his campaign and cabinet, Putin must recognize them for what they are: a personal politburo made up of family members and loyalists. There are folks like Michael Flynn, who sat next to Putin at a 2015 gala in Moscow to celebrate a state-sponsored TV network, and received $33,750 to deliver a Russian-friendly speech. Trump will name Flynn, his fiercest attack dog on the campaign trail, as his National Security Advisor, before firing him three weeks later, purportedly for lying about his contacts with Russian officials.

Jared Kushner, Trump's 36-year-old son-in-law, serves as a top advisor, despite also having met with Russian officials. His resume includes a partnership with an Israeli firm notorious for bribery, which would appear to violate the Foreign Corrupt Practices Act. Kushner has no experience as a public servant, so naturally Trump assigns him to broker Middle East peace, cure the opioid addiction crisis, and reinvent government.

Nobody really believes Kushner will do any of this. But then, nobody really believes anything Trump says. There is no past or future, no global strategy, or mission, just a relentless prowling from conflict to compliment with no binding ethical oversight. When it becomes clear the Trump tax plan will net the president up to a billion dollars, nobody bats an eyelash.

Putin sees all of this. As a student of the Cold War, maybe he's seen it coming for years, the phony populism of Reagan collapsing under the weight of plutocratic policy, the calculated indoctrination of conservatives, the decadence of a left more devoted to self-actualization than activism, the phony utopian patter of tech companies hawking screen addiction as communalism.

For decades, American politicians used the Soviet Union as a foil, the Totalitarian Other invoked to instill a sense of unity and pride in the population. The Cold War spurred a widespread embrace of scientific progress and human rights. Americans were defenders of freedom, exporters of liberty whose moral superiority ordained their defeat of Communism. With the Soviet threat gone, American nationalism lost focus. The rise of Islamic terrorism rekindled a sense of global heroism. But the central byproduct of the "War on Terror" was a war sold on disinformation, an open embrace of torture, a growing climate of fear.

Watching from afar, Putin can see the American experiment in self-governance imploding. Its leaders are no longer statesmen, but power-mad courtiers, entertainers, and spoiled scions of wealth. Pundits have replaced journalists. Citizens, rebranded as taxpayers, retreat into apathy and cynicism, the distractions of amusement. A lot of things have to break right for his man to win. But Putin sees how much already has broken that Trump would have a chance.

◆ ◆ ◆

Remember: Putin is playing the long game. He knows that the fall of the Soviet Union ushered in a wave of global liberalism, in which democracies spiked from a couple of dozen to a hundred worldwide. But he has also seen that wave recede in recent years, as more and more countries revert to authoritarianism. The Chinese crush a democratic rebellion. Autocrats come to power in Turkey, Hungary, Poland, the Philippines, and Indonesia. The hopes of the Arab spring dissolve into sectarian violence. Even within the great states of Western Europe—France, Netherlands—a crude ethnic nationalism takes root.

This is why Putin views Trump as the ultimate Russian asset. Because his entire pitch is an assault on liberal democracy: on the free press, on science and reason, on political civility and public integrity. He doesn't have the attention span or intellect to be a true authoritarian. He can't have journalists or judges killed. But every day, in the eyes of the world, Trump degrades democracy.

For years, Putin has been telling his own people a story about America. That it's a land of self-righteous braggarts and hypocrites, drunk on false virtues but decaying from within. Trump's ascendance proves him right. The U.S. is no more enlightened than any other country. Its citizens can be brainwashed. Its civic institutions, rotted by greed, will only hasten the downfall.

Whether or not they ever shook on it, Trump and Putin made a deal. But only Putin apprehended its true terms. If Trump were defeated, conservatives would feel a deep sense of betrayal, one that would fester until the next Trump came along. But a Trump win would send America into an even more calamitous spiral, the one Richard Hofstadter described at the apex of the Cold War: "This demand for total triumph leads to the formulation of hopelessly unrealistic goals, and since these goals are not even remotely attainable, failure constantly heightens the paranoid's sense of frustration. Even partial success leaves him with the same feeling of powerlessness with which he began, and this in turn only strengthens his awareness of the vast and terrifying quality of the enemy he opposes."

Putin knew he could never win the Cold War alone. He needed our help.

ONE FINAL BAD STORY

AMERICA IS INCAPABLE
OF MORAL IMPROVEMENT

As I write this, the new president has been in office for a year. He has sought to make good on an agenda that satisfies the wish lists of his corporate sponsors (massive deregulation) and his base (Muslim bans, deportations). He endorsed an astonishingly cruel and senseless health care bill, signed a massive tax cut for corporate America, and stocked the judiciary with reactionary ideologues. We now know that his campaign at least attempted to conspire with a hostile foreign power to win the election, and that he will obstruct the investigation into this treason at any cost.

He stocked his cabinet with a consortium of feckless plutocrats, many of whom appear driven to raze the departments and agencies they run. Environmental protection, diplomacy, civil rights, free trade, public education, health care—all are hurtling toward that familiar Trumpian terminus: bankruptcy. Meanwhile, the markets for white supremacy, mass shootings, corporate profiteering, and nuclear cataclysm are booming.

His personal conduct remains an adolescent psychodrama: popularity mongering, conspiracy mongering, Twitter mongering, the tireless projection of his mongering onto perceived enemies. His aides and allies are mortified by his cognitive deterioration, his inability to read, or concentrate. It becomes more and more obvious that he's unfit for the office. And yet the office belongs to him.

The press has begun to take him more seriously, if only because he now possesses the power not just to spike ratings but to destroy lives. But the networks continue to fall for the same tricks over and over, dispatching pundits to howl over what he says rather than allowing journalists to explain what he has done, and intends to do. Cable anchors continue to marvel at his ability to "change the conversation" without acknowledging that they are the ones changing the conversation.

And all the while, the president's balance sheet, hidden from public view, swells with foreign favors—Chinese patents, hotel suites awash in sheiks, Russians snapping up condos—a racket so flagrant as to make Nixon's deal with dairy farmers seem demur. For now, Trump operates within a familiar pocket of privilege, cosseted by the healthy economy he inherited and congressional allies whose legislative ambitions require them to ignore his impeachable corruptions.

The investigation by special counsel Robert Mueller, launched after the president's sacking of Comey, continues to lay bare the web of corruption and lies that marks Trump-world as something closer to a mafia operation than a presidential administration. And yet, even if Mueller presents definitive proof that a sitting president colluded with Russia and obstructed justice, it is not clear—as it was during Watergate—that he will be removed from office. Meaning that the only real limits on his power, aside from the courts, are his own ineptitude, inattention, and sloth. He has the heart of an autocrat but the mind of a gorilla.

No one knows what Trump will do if there is, for instance, a large-scale terrorist attack on U.S. soil, or a provocation engineered by a foreign enemy, or even large-scale protests in American cities, whether he will heed the rational voices in his orbit or those eager to activate his despotic impulses. We can say only two things with assurance: that innocent people will get hurt, and that it will never be his fault.

♦ ♦ ♦

My literary hero, Kurt Vonnegut, didn't live long enough to see Trump barnstorm through the Rust Belt swing states. But Vonnegut foresaw the underlying dynamics at those events with ruthless precision. "It is in fact a crime for an American to be poor, even though America is a nation of poor," he observed in *Slaughterhouse Five*. "Every other nation has folk traditions of men who were poor but extremely wise and virtuous, and therefore more estimable than anyone with power and gold. No such tales are told by the American poor. They mock themselves and glorify their betters. . . . This inward blame has been a treasure for the rich and powerful, who have had to do less for their poor, publicly and privately, than any other ruling class since, say, Napoleonic times."

And I think, too, about guys like Robert Mercer (candidate Trump's patron) who used a talent for financial computation to amass billions and has chosen to invest in an ideology that sanctifies his fortune, and depicts those in poverty as worthless. This mindset, a precise repudiation of the Beatitudes, proudly displays the moral logic of eugenics. It is the wet dream of capitalism tumbling into the nightmare of fascism.

It is also the inexhaustible story of class, of Gatsby, "the colossal vitality of his illusion," and of the man who vanquishes him, Tom Buchanan. "I couldn't forgive him or like him," Nick Carraway tells us, "but I saw that what he had done was, to him, entirely justified. It was all very careless and confused. They were careless people, Tom and Daisy—they smashed up things and creatures and then retreated back into their money or their vast carelessness, or whatever it was that kept them together, and let other people clean up the mess they had made."

◆ ◆ ◆

Do you see the story? Do you see anything? It seems to me I am trying to tell you a dream.

That is Marlow, struggling to convey the horrors of his expedition. And it is how I feel for much of my waking life, how many Americans feel, as we attempt to understand and absorb the unstable aggression of this new president. "He struggled with himself too. I saw it,—I heard it. I saw the inconceivable mystery of a soul that knew no restraint, no faith, and no fear, yet struggling blindly with itself."

The vitality of his delusion is precisely what makes Kurtz so hypnotizing. "I was fascinated," Marlow confesses. "It was as though a veil had been rent. I saw on that ivory face the expression of sombre pride, of ruthless power, of craven terror—of an intense and hopeless despair." Men of desperate action have long ruled the American imagination. And yet their strength, as Conrad reminds us, is just an accident arising from the weakness of others.

◆ ◆ ◆

We are remitted, time and again, to the province of Ahab, the gasping ruin of that final scene, the mad captain taken under by his quarry, the young orphan who served him, who lives to tell the tale only by holding fast to a casket of American wood. How bad will it get? How much of our common good, our decency, will we surrender? To what extent are we to blame for this outcome? And what are we to do now that it is upon us?

◆ ◆ ◆

In the novel *The Visit of the Royal Physician* by the Swedish writer Per Olov Enquist, a German doctor named Struensee is summoned to the court of the mad Danish king and winds up importing the Enlightenment to the "filthy little country" of Denmark. He abolishes cronyism and torture, funds hospitals, and grants citizens unprecedented freedoms. But Struensee has a fatal flaw, one his lover, the queen, spots instantly. "She had felt a unique pleasure when she understood for the first time that she could instill terror. But he did not. There was something fundamentally wrong with him," she observes. "Why was it always the wrong people who were chosen to do good?"

I thought about this question a great deal during the Obama era, as he courted enemies bent on his destruction, as he declined to prosecute the criminal avarice of Wall Street executives, as he extended the Bush tax cuts and, in particular, as news emerged that he knew, months before the election, of the FBI investigation into collusion between the Trump campaign and Russia.

Because Struensee lacks the will necessary to purge the court, its reactionary forces naturally rise up to destroy him.

"Then the spark was ignited everywhere, and the masses poured out: the poor, those who had never dreamed of a revolution but were now offered the comfort of violence, without punishment, without meaning. They revolted, but with no purpose other than the excuse of purity."

The novel asks whether noble ideas alone are enough to improve the world, or whether bloodshed is the necessary price of moral progress. A quick survey of American history doesn't offer much room for hope. Our nation was forged in war, expanded by means of an energetic genocide, and liberated from the sin of slavery at the price of half a million souls. Struensee, by contrast, attempts to legislate equality and tolerance by decree, from the safety of a royal den.

At the height of his influence, the Royal Physician decides to take the King on a tour of the countryside, so that he can see the conditions his people endure. At dusk, they spot a severely beaten teenage serf, seated on a wooden trestle. Struensee jumps out of the royal coach, hoping to secure a pardon for the boy. But a mob of peasants approaches and he panics: "Reason, rules, titles, or power had no authority in this wilderness. Here the people were animals. They would tear him limb from limb." Struensee has the purest of motives, but he mistrusts the people he hopes to save.

◆ ◆ ◆

A version of this mindset animates both sides of our present divide. We now know that many voters, especially older whites, haunted by the terror attacks of 2001 and a rising demographic tide, are willing to see the rights of Muslims, immigrants, and people of color abrogated. But so, too, there are Americans who look upon these abrogaters as an unruly mob, impervious to moral logic, angry, armed, and dangerous.

As we sort ourselves into like-minded communities, both online and off, the divide widens. Politicians and media executives, marketers and algorithmists, mine this division for profit, presenting visions of the "other side" so monstrous that we retreat into the psychic comfort of our own righteousness. One of my journalism students captured the crisis quite succinctly, in the form of a question: "What do you do if, no matter what you write, the reader won't believe you?"

I thought about how new the precepts of the enlightenment (science, reason, equality) are within the flickering span of human history. Perhaps the regression of our Fourth Estate is just the visible symptom of some much deeper moral regression in the body politic, a return to ancient superstitions. Perhaps we yearned for a style of leadership that rejected enlightenment altogether, that affirmed our primitive impulses. Perhaps we authored a story in which the resurrection of the American spirit required the shuttering of the American mind.

Or perhaps I should have told my student this: that the essential commodity of journalism, like religion, is the mirage of certainty. This mirage appears most obviously in the demagoguery of talk radio, but dwells also within the self-congratulating pieties of the left. As a people, we are besieged by doubt, and therefore desperate to construct a world free from our tormentor.

In the introduction to his piercing essay collection, *Loitering*, Charles D'Ambrosio describes what it feels like, as a recovering journalist, to withstand such discourse. "In a leveling climate of summations," he observes, "crowded with public figures who speak exclusively from positions of final authority, issuing an endless stream of conclusions, I get a wary sense in my gut of a world that's making its appeal to my indolence and emptiness, asking only for surrender."

That's how most of us feel. But we conceal our uncertainty "in shame, or something of that character, feeling isolated and singular, useless and a little vulnerable." Like D'Ambrosio, we suppress the disquieting truth "that we are more intimately bound to one another by our kindred doubts than our brave conclusions."

◆ ◆ ◆

The fate of America, and of the species, now depends on our ability to solve crises that are beyond empirical doubt: climate change, resource depletion, inequalities of wealth and opportunity, all of which are triggering mass migrations, political unrest, and violent extremism. We can begin to solve these crises only if we reject bad stories and place our faith in reason and empiricism.

Rising against all this—Enlightenment 2.0, you might call it—comes a familiar tide of dogma, marked by reactionary fervor, a scorn of science, the privileging of faith above fact, and blunt appeals to savagery.

In politics, it has taken the form of a ruthless free market theology, a make-believe retreat from globalism, a nostalgia for white hegemony camouflaged in enraged nationalism. But this style of thought isn't restricted to our political discourse. It has become the default setting of a culture that lurches about within the shadow of its own extinction yet lacks the moral imagination to change its destiny.

Trace this conflict back a few millennia and we arrive at the dividing line between prophetic literature and apocalyptic writing. Isaiah and Jeremiah preached an angry gospel but promised deliverance. They wanted to rescue their nation before it was too late. Apocalyptic writers deemed the world beyond repair, and looked to a future in which paradise for the select would be achieved only by upheaval.

You can see this mindset at work among the tech billionaires prepping their luxury bunkers for nuclear winter or plague, and among citizens like my mother-in-law, a woman barely clinging to the middle-class, in declining health, whose creed consists of stories told by Fox News and the Catholic Church, who despises Obamacare and Planned Parenthood but does not fear global warming, or even death, which will empanel her soul in the ultimate luxury bunker.

I say this not to mock my mother-in-law's faith. Only to stress that her interests extend beyond her soul. She has three grandchildren, the youngest of whom is four years old. All three will have to live on this Earth. The quality of their lives will depend on whether enough of the adults around them can turn away from celestial fatalism and toward the enormity of our earthly tasks.

Surveying the ruin of his schemes, Struensee is left to wonder: "Was that what a human being was? Both an opportunity and a black torch?"

♦ ♦ ♦

Not long ago, my wife and I saw *Moonlight*, a film that manages to capture—far more vividly than I was able, in my account of the Canyon—the hidden lives of boys in neighborhoods such as Liberty City. Because we see movies in the theater so rarely, our kids naturally wanted to know what *Moonlight* was about. And so we set about trying to explain how difficult it can be to grow up gay, especially if you are an African-American boy living in poverty.

Our son Jude, who is eight, had a rather striking reaction, which he whacked out on the ancient typewriter we recently gave him. It read as follows:

Gay meens happy

That is grammatically correct.

That does not have ANYTHING to do with gender, racism, or anything. Gay people could easily be called happy people. And then there is the truth that Gay people are just happyer than us. There is no way someone would go raise taxes just for them right? That has all been proven wrong by our leader, who has gone against happy people. Now the people WHO are really married to the same gender are called people.

That is grammatically correct.

Jude's objection here was to our modern usage of the word "gay." But the more I studied this note, the more convinced I became that he was lodging an emotional complaint—about the manner in which the election had embittered our national and domestic mood.

Throughout the campaign, we tried to keep our kids focused on positive goals: distributing wealth more fairly, battling global warming, electing our first female president. But they're not dumb. You can sort of hide stupid from a second grader; you can't hide mean. In the months since the election, the kids have seen us muttering darkly, getting upset more often, arguing.

What Jude picked up on was the visceral sense that the big winner in 2016 was a politics of despair and division, the feeling that one side can be happy only if another side is sad, that there is no collective hope.

"How's all that hopey-changey stuff working out for ya?"

This smirking query, posed a few years back by Sarah Palin, strikes at the heart of our republic. What happens when we treat hope as a sucker's game? When policy goals are eclipsed by the exaltation of grievance, a desire to exhaust, confound, and dispirit? You can turn on cable television at any hour of the day and watch professionals being paid to mangle hope. Bucky Dunn is on right now.

There's a reason Trumpism derived so much vampiric energy from its abuse of immigrants: because immigrants possess what must be, particularly for those who feel their own horizons dimming, an unbearably hopeful vision of America. *That has all been proven wrong by our leader, who has gone against happy people.*

◆ ◆ ◆

The longer I spend on the planet, the more convinced I become that children exist not just to perpetuate our DNA, or replenish our faith in the species, but to remind us of the power vested in stories.

For the past year, I've been telling our four-year-old Rosalie stories about a little girl named Posalie, who goes on various hyperglycemic adventures with her best friend, Pipsqueak the Penguin. They spend a lot of time with Chocolatte, the God of the Chocolate Volcano, and recently, guided by a golden hummingbird named Eggbert, they journeyed to the center of the Earth, which they discovered was not made of iron and nickel but salt water taffy, predominantly the chocolate kind with a blurry dab of cherry in the middle.

Rosalie, who can be a little bossy, routinely calls out warnings and instructions to Posalie. She recently pressed herself against my chest, where she understood Posalie to live, and was thrilled when Posalie reported being able to see her face over the clouds. The two of them were soon having lengthy and urgent conversations, whisper-screaming questions and answers at each other, as you would in a cave.

A few months ago, my wife had to have surgery and spend a night in the hospital. Rosalie appeared unfazed by her absence, though at bedtime she called out to Posalie to explain the situation and asked if Posalie would come out of my chest and snuggle with her.

I paused for a long moment. "Posalie's already asleep."

"We can wake her up," Rosalie replied, quite reasonably.

"But her mommy and daddy will worry if she's not there."

Rosalie's face froze, then her chin started to tremble, followed by the rest of her. I could see at once all the fear she'd been holding in about her mommy. "Why can't she come *now*?" she said, and broke down sobbing.

◆ ◆ ◆

I've been trying to keep this moment in mind amid all the calculated deceit enveloping us. People believe what they need to believe. Our stories about the world arise from the panic of our inner lives. Beneath all our lesser defenses—the swirling rage and paranoia and indifference—are human beings somehow in pain.

The question before us now is whether enough of us can confront our bad stories and divine their meaning, and begin to tell better ones. "Not everything that is faced can be changed," as James Baldwin reminds us. "But nothing can be changed until it is faced." How did so many of us come to believe that hatred would lead to rebirth? Or that elections don't matter? Or that America will endure regardless of our misbehavior?

In this version of the story, America is the Prodigal Son, wayward at times but always returning home to feast on the fattened calves of the family estate. It's a myth we cling to because the alternative is simply too bleak: that our style of capitalism has, under the guise of democracy, acted as a financial centrifuge, perhaps the most brutal aggregator of wealth in human history, built on a foundation of slave labor and fortified by plunder, imperial warfare, the decimation of the labor movement, the predation of Wall Street, the steady subjugation of public oversight to private gain. Greed and self-interest do not fade away as a natural function of evolution, nor at the direction of Christian mercy.

If there is a status quo to protect, it resides with those who control the nation's wealth and have devised a political system in which that wealth serves as an instrument of raw power. Any reformation must therefore begin by dismantling these mechanisms.

Americans of all stripes clamor about wanting to believe in our electoral system. Why not target the glaring procedural defects: campaign finance, gerrymandering, the Electoral College, voter suppression? Of these issues, only the last is a matter of dispute, and the basis of that dispute is a racist fantasia about "voter fraud" that even Republican voting officials admit is false.

Reform in these areas is unlikely to come from members of our political or media class. Too many people make too much money off the current system. But if our citizenry is truly sick of the special interests, the lobbyists, the PACs and negative ads, the mechanics of corporate influence, if they're sick of political lines being drawn by partisans and campaigns conducted exclusively in swing states and votes being weighted differently, then citizens must become a lobby, must push for laws that bleed money from politics and unrig our elections. This lobby should consist of nearly every citizen of this country who is not a billionaire, a demagogue, a network executive, a pollster, a consultant, or a politician.

We just obediently handed 100 percent of the presidency to a candidate who received three million votes fewer than his opponent, from barely 25 percent of the eligible voters. The same thing would be true if Clinton had won. Is that the story of a democracy? Or a tyranny of the elites?

◆ ◆ ◆

None of these notions is new. They amount to a revival of what Teddy Roosevelt proposed in his famous New National-ism Speech of 1910. The former president argued that human welfare should be valued above property rights, and that the federal government should safeguard social justice against corporate greed.

The platform he outlined included a National Health Service, social insurance for the elderly and needy, an eight-hour workday, a minimum wage, worker's compensation, farm relief, an inheritance tax, a federal income tax, a securities commission. His political reforms included suffrage for women and the direct election of Senators, who were at that time selected by state legislatures. He also called for strict

limits on campaign contributions, the registration of lobbyists, and the recording of all Congressional proceedings, "to
destroy this invisible Government, to dissolve the unholy alliance between corrupt business and corrupt politics."

Roosevelt sought to defend the founding principle of
America: equality of opportunity. "In the struggle for this
great end, nations rise from barbarism to civilization, and
through it people press forward from one stage of enlightenment to the next," he observed. "At many stages in the advance
of humanity, this conflict between the men who possess more
than they have earned and the men who have earned more
than they possess is the central condition of progress. In our
day it appears as the struggle of freemen to gain and hold the
right of self-government as against the special interests, who
twist the methods of free government into machinery for de-
feating the popular will. At every stage, and under all circum-
stances, the essence of the struggle is to equalize opportunity,
destroy privilege, and give to the life and citizenship of every
individual the highest possible value both to himself and to
the commonwealth. That is nothing new. All I ask in civil life
is what you fought for in the Civil War."

♦ ♦ ♦

There has been much talk since the election of The Resistance,
an umbrella term meant to signify the forces aligned against

the new administration and its interests. But if we're serious about our democracy, we need to take up a more fundamental reformation, of the sort that Roosevelt envisioned.

This will require us to confront our underlying habits of thought and feeling. Nearly half our voting population doesn't bother to exercise its franchise. Another quarter consistently votes against its interests. It doesn't matter how many of our fellow political junkies we get to "like" our latest online offering if we cannot awaken the sleeping giant of our democracy: the apathetic.

We must also change our relationship toward the Fourth Estate. If we want media corporations to treat democracy as something more than an entertainment product, we have to do so first. We can't keep consuming politics like a sporting event or a farce. The more we watch pundits yelling at each other, the more the networks will show us pundits yelling at each other. The more we watch experts explaining the effects of policy on citizens, the more the networks will show us experts explaining the effects of policy on citizens. It's that simple.

You can't advocate for serious discourse and simultaneously participate in the trivialization of discourse. Or rather, you can. But the story is going to end badly.

◆ ◆ ◆

When the filter through which we view the world privileges propaganda over reportage, the inevitable result is an erosion in our public standards of truth and decency. The men and women in charge of our media filter face a moral impasse. Do they want to operate as a free press or a for-profit corporation? Is their core product information or inflammation?

"If ever there was a people ripe for dictatorship it is the American people today. Should a homegrown Hitler appear, whose voice, amongst the public orders, would be raised against him in derision? Certainly no voice on television: 'Sorry, the guy has a lot of fans. Sure, we know he's bad news, but you can't hurt people's feelings. They buy soap, too.'" Gore Vidal wrote that in 1958.

Nearly six decades later, Les Moonves, the chairman of CBS, ratified this view, not with shame but a businessman's unctuous wink. Sociopaths and demagogues sell more soap than newsmen, so give them their turn at the mic. Bad news for the country remains banner news for the shareholders.

The same philosophy infects insta-moguls such as Mark Zuckerberg, who allowed Facebook to become a sewer of disinformation during the campaign. If he and the other titans of social media want their tech-utopian happy talk taken seriously, they can start by taking some personal responsibility for their sites and cracking down on the agitprop cranked out by Albanian propaganda farms, which their bloodless algorithms so efficiently promote.

I imagine the bad story Zuckerberg tells himself at night these days is that his failure to do so represented a defense of free speech. The real story is that he wants market share, even if it comes at the expense of democratic integrity. As for Moonves, he tells himself that he is merely recording the decline of our Republic, like the Greek historian Tacitus who documented the atrocities of Nero. But history will not record Moonves as Tacitus. He will be the fiddle Nero played while Rome burned.

◆ ◆ ◆

We are all products of the stories we live, the ones drawn from our memories, the ones our parents tell us, the ones inflicted upon us by the world. Our children are the stories we send out into the world.

When I was four years old, my parents sat my two brothers and me down and told us a strange story. My father, they said, was going to link arms with some friends and block the road leading to a nearby air force base, so vehicles couldn't go in or out. Dad was doing this to protest the war in Vietnam, but it was illegal and he might wind up in jail. This was just months after the 1968 Democratic Convention, at which the National Guard had bloodied hundreds of protestors, and those scenes must have been on his mind, because he later confessed to me that he was shaking when the police descended upon him.

My mother's political awakening was a more complicated business. Her parents, Irving and Annie Rosenthal, grew up during the Great Depression and perhaps because of what they saw, they came to believe that the bounty of the Earth should be divided more or less equally among its inhabitants. This was a dangerous view to hold during the 1950s, and Annie, who taught at PS 113 in Harlem, and later became an assistant principal there, was eventually asked to testify before the New York City Board of Education. This was all part of the work done by the House Committee on Un-American Affairs, championed by Joseph McCarthy and his protégé Roy Cohn. In the end, Annie didn't testify. She took an early retirement instead. She was lucky, compared to a lot of other folks.

As a child, my mother never knew her parents were Communists. They concealed the extent of their involvement to keep their daughters out of danger. The weekly meetings they attended were passed off as social gatherings. Irving published articles under a pseudonym. What they couldn't hide was a pervasive sense of anxiety around politics.

Toward the end of her life, my mom wrote a short memoir about growing up as a red-diaper baby in the Bronx. She knew the country was heading in a dark direction and she felt called to speak about her own experiences.

One story that never made it into that manuscript took place when she was just a young girl. It had haunted her ever since. She played piano quite seriously in her youth, and one day she was practicing a Mozart sonata in her family's tiny apartment. Her dad began arguing about politics with his brother Saul. The dispute grew loud then angry and my mom found herself getting more and more upset until finally she stopped playing altogether and began, instead, to weep.

Her father turned to her, bewildered. "What's wrong?" he said. "We were just having a discussion."

◆ ◆ ◆

This was one of the last stories my mother ever told me. It is how America feels to me these days: a beautiful song drowned out by shouting.

◆ ◆ ◆

Like many red-diaper babies, my mother was obsessed with the trial and execution of Julius and Ethel Rosenberg, suspected Russian spies who were sent to the electric chair. My mom had just turned fifteen when they were killed and she had, by then, sussed out the true nature of her parents' political beliefs. She carried this fear through her life. But she never allowed it to disable her decency. In college, she and two other white classmates went with a group of African-American students to a local restaurant in Southern Ohio and insisted upon being served—in accordance with the law but against the customs of this particular establishment. She and my father both marched for Civil Rights and against the war in Vietnam.

These were the stories I heard as a kid. I understood them to mean that moral progress comes at the cost of personal sacrifice, sometimes in the face of armed resistance, that we are summoned to this sacrifice despite our own fears, at those moments when a greater cause activates the individual conscience.

My parents believed in the America that gave women the vote and immigrants a refuge and fought to end slavery and segregation. They were hippies of an upwardly mobile sort, idealists who took us to live, briefly, on a commune. The next summer, as you'll recall, Nixon was chased from office, and a spirit of bruised idealism and reform flourished.

♦ ♦ ♦

On the day after the election, I went swimming with my son Jude. We were in Florida, at a writing conference, and on the way to the hotel pool I spotted a young father with his daughter, who looked to be about three. She was seated on the chaise lounge next to her dad, happily munching on potato chips.

"Let's not have any more snacks," the dad said, "It's going to be dinner soon."

The girl continued to feed chips into her mouth, at a slightly greater clip.

"Good luck with that," I said to the dad ruefully, as I passed by.

He laughed and we felt that instant kinship shared by fathers of young, iron-willed daughters against whom we know ourselves to be essentially powerless.

Some minutes later, my son pulled me to his side in the shallow end. "Look at that man," he whispered. "Look at what he's wearing."

I glanced up and saw the young father with whom I'd just shared a moment of levity, a bright red *Make America Great Again* hat perched on his head.

Jude wanted me to react with horror, or at least indignation. But I had no idea what stories had led this guy to put on that hat. I knew only that he was a father, like me, an American on vacation and at the mercy of his lovely daughter. To make any further judgment about him would be a failure of moral imagination. We're suffering from enough of that already.

The real question, then, is what stories guide our fellow citizens? How have these stories led so many to squander their franchise? To accept the idea that we can be united by those who sow discord, or made great without admitting what, in our weakest moments, we are? Amid the constant prod of monetized distraction, can we slow down and start to connect the dots between our compulsive consumption of entertainment and the degradation of our public discourse, between the bread and circuses and the corrupt leaders? Can we activate what Foster Wallace called the "deep need to believe"?

If we're ever going to get out of this mess, we can no longer fritter away our passion on tribal contempt. We have to fight in a new way. We have to be the fools in charge of forgiveness.

◆ ◆ ◆

A century ago, William Butler Yeats composed "The Second Coming," whose famous opening stanza concludes:

> The blood-dimmed tide is loosed, and everywhere
> The ceremony of innocence is drowned;
> The best lack all conviction, while the worst
> Are full of passionate intensity.

These lines, summoned in response to the atrocity of World War I, are a vital, if unsettling, reminder that humans inevitably struggle through cycles of terror and violent upheaval. Every epoch heralds its own rough beast slouching toward Bethlehem.

There is some evidence to suggest that Americans are revising their political attitudes, coming to view democracy as a more participatory arrangement, calling for vigilance and activism. But to stem the tide of cruelty in this country, to overcome the fatal "passivity and egoism" Huxley warned of, I believe we must also embrace a deeper and more personal form of resistance.

We must resist what the poet Wallace Stevens referred to as "the pressure of the real," the manner in which our souls become desensitized by the grim and unending procession of accounts we call news. We mustn't succumb to a panic that robs us of our imagination, our capacity to contemplate and wonder and invent.

It's not enough just to fight bad stories. If that's all we do, we will become trapped in a reactive cycle, debunking one outrage after another, with no greater mission than mitigation. We have to be able to dream up stories that offer a vision of the American spirit as one of kindness and decency, the sort that powered the Emancipation Proclamation and the New Deal and the War on Poverty.

Joseph Conrad, so famous for peering into our heart of darkness, never lost his great faith in the act storytelling, and the pursuit of art more broadly. Scientists and thinkers, he observed, make their appeal "to those qualities . . . that fit us best for the hazardous enterprise of living." The artist, by contrast, "speaks to our capacity for delight and wonder, to the sense of mystery surrounding our lives, to our sense of pity, and beauty, and pain; to the latent feeling of fellowship with all creation—and to the subtle but invincible conviction of solidarity . . . in dreams, in joy, in sorrow, in aspirations, in illusions, in hope, in fear, which binds men to each other, which binds together all humanity—the dead to the living and the living to the unborn."

◆ ◆ ◆

The story of America is, in some ways, quite simple. We were a nation borne of high ideals and low behaviors, the land of *all men are created equal* and slave labor. We've been engaged in a pitched struggle ever since, between greed and generosity, between the comforts of ignorance and the burden of moral knowledge. Nobody knows how the story ends because we haven't written it yet. We know only that it belongs to us: our actions, our convictions, our doubts. We can pretend that we live apart from those who suffer, that we owe them nothing. But I can't think of a single story—at least not one I could find in a church, one I would read to my children—that accords with this view.

◆ ◆ ◆

A few years back, I went on the radio to talk about *The Grapes of Wrath*, John Steinbeck's novel about the mass migration that besieged America during the Great Depression. I said just about what you would expect: that it was a brave and beautiful novel, that Steinbeck wanted Americans to question why we tolerate avarice, why we so often side with the mighty and turn our backs on the meek, and that he wanted his readers to recognize what he had witnessed as a journalist: that our government can and does act as a force for good in the lives of the disenfranchised.

I received a few responses to the segment, but the one I remember most vividly came from a man who insisted that, while he understood the book was a classic, its final scene had always disgusted him. The book ends, of course, with the Joad daughter, Rose of Sharon, giving birth to a stillborn child in a barn where she has sought shelter from a storm. Also in the barn is an emaciated stranger. The final lines read:

> Then slowly she lay down beside him. He shook his head slowly from side to side. Rose of Sharon loosened one side of the blanket and bared her breast. 'You got to,' she said. She squirmed closer and pulled his head close. 'There!' she said. 'There.' Her hand moved behind his head and supported it. Her finger moved gently in his hair. She looked up and across the barn, and her lips came together and smiled mysteriously.